TRIAL BUY VACUUM

My earliest memories of the vacuum I sold are of that same machine in my parents' home when I was growing up. When I was told it was a life time machine I believed it unfortunately I also then believed a lot of stuff I shouldn't have.

THE BEGINNING

At the beginning of this embarkation I had 3 years of intense sales pressure and a decent amount of knowledge of the sales cycle. This was from a call center where I toiled after a previous job which was seasonal that had ended and I came back from a 10 month stint in Europe. So I started searching for employment elsewhere after learning that it was possible the contact center was going to have another dramatic cutback of hours which meant jobs. So I applied at more than one place and then one day at work my phone rings and it was a person who did telemarketing for the owner of the business and she booked me for an interview. I had the interview with the business owner and he told me he had to fax my resume to head office and they would get back,(imagine my shock years later when I'm doing the interview and he just puts the resumes on the desk and says we'll call them all for tomorrow). The next day at work my phone rings and it's the owner of the company telling me my training starts on Monday and to be there for it. I said well first I need to give 2 weeks' notice to my current employer and I recall vividly the lie "there won't be another training class for 6 months". I jumped and resigned as a supervisor and remained on as a representative to help with the numbers at the contact center for a bit. As luck would unfortunately happen that center closed 6 months after I resigned permanently. (which I had no choice in doing if I was too keep selling vacuums because the sales territory I was hired for had moved 100-140km away which meant moon lighting was no longer an option). The center closed and many people were out of work in the capital city my home.

This closure was used by the person who owns the

establishment where I was employed in attempting to recruit other individuals banking on the company's history from 1928 or so, as being a long time company that never closes sure sounds decent. It's likely true however as I come to find out later on there was more inaccuracies then truths in more than less of what was presented. As I mentioned it was not great because I was a supervisor in the call center and there was a team which varied between 12 and 30 people whom I was responsible for at various times. When he used my name it carried some weight for some people. Never of course did he ask permission to use me in such a manner and I like everyone else who was sold on the dream of owning their own little independent franchise would have not had a problem with it.

This is a real story though I wish it were a fantasy or a nightmare however this is my story about the situation I found myself in and how I tried to get out multiple times but got sucked back in for the carrot, which at the end of the day vanished. And how it brought financial ruin to me and my wife for a period of time and may have had a significant impact on my mental health.

THE INTERVIEW

    For my interview I arrived at the office, I was greeted by Chelsea and she told me to have a seat and that Mr Tahhan would be with me shortly so I did, everything looked professional in the office. There was no hint of the horrors Id soon be facing, from wondering if I would make my mortgage payment and power bill that month. Which was a change from having the utilities paid 1-2 months in advance as I had done prior to working for this company. Mr Tahhan comes out of the office and greets me I shake his hand it's a firm hand shake with a intent in his eyes. He says come in and I follow him into his office for the interview. There is one unit which I would be tasked to sell in the office, the air purifier unit not the vacuum unit. For the interview there is a series of slides either on a computer or in a book where the pages get flipped, the following are the 12 of them.

INTERVIEW SLIDE SHOW

Healthy Living Home Ltd.

Fredericton, New Brunswick / Regional Office
ASSOCIATED WITH THE
CANAIDAN DIVISION OF HMI

HMI INDUSTRIES – 1928

- WORLD HEADQUARTERS IN CLEVELAND, OH
- 75+ YEARS HISTORY (NO STRIKES, LAYOFFS OR INTERUPTIONS IN SERVICE)
- TRADED OVER THE COUNTER
- (AAAA-2) RATING WITH DUNN ^ BRADSTREET
- RAPID GRPWTH WORLDWIDE
- 65+ COUNTRIES
- PRESIDENT"E" CERTIFICATE

MAJOR MANUFACTURER OF HEALTH
& AIR FILTRATION PRODUCTS
Medi-pure

- MEDI-FILTER / HISHEST LEVEL OF
- FILTRATION ON THE MARKET

Qualifications

- Self Disciplined
- 18 Years of Age
- Bondable
- Home Phone
- Reliable Transportation
- Minimum 1 year Residency

PRODUCTS
Medi - Pure Air Filtration

*Highest Level of Filtration Available on the Market

*Recommended by Allergists, and Dr. Loughridge M.D. Author of "Every Breath you Take" and Olympic Gold Medallist Tom Dolan

TRIAL BUY VACUUM

Position

CUSTOMER SERVICE
Indoor Air Quality Systems Associate

- **Set Up & Display Department**
- **Consulting**
- **Marketing**
- **Order Taking and Delivery**

Company Structure

- **Management**
  Training and Coordinating Depts.
- **IAQS Associate Dept**
  Live commercial with Clientele
- **Appointment Scheduling Dept**
  Schedules appointments for IAQS Associates
- **Customer Service Dept.**
  Servicing Clients

Pay Structure

12 Displays per Week

X $30.00

= $360.00

Minimum of 48 hours Notice for Day off.
- **Dress Code**
  Clean, Neat & Professional
- **Territory**
  Maximum 50-60 Kilometer of Office

Benefits

- Yearly Bonuses

- Free Product and Field orientation

- Incentive Bonuses

- Advanced Company Training

- Profit Sharing

- Guaranteed Opportunity for Advancement

TRIAL BUY VACUUM

 **Advancement**

- **Crew Chief**
- **Assistant Manager**
- **Manager**
- **Regional Distributor**
- **Senior Regional Distributor**
- **Master Distributor**
- **Premier Master Distributor**
- **Corporate**

 **Office Policies**

- **Working Hours**
  Monday to Saturday
  Full Time starts at 10am

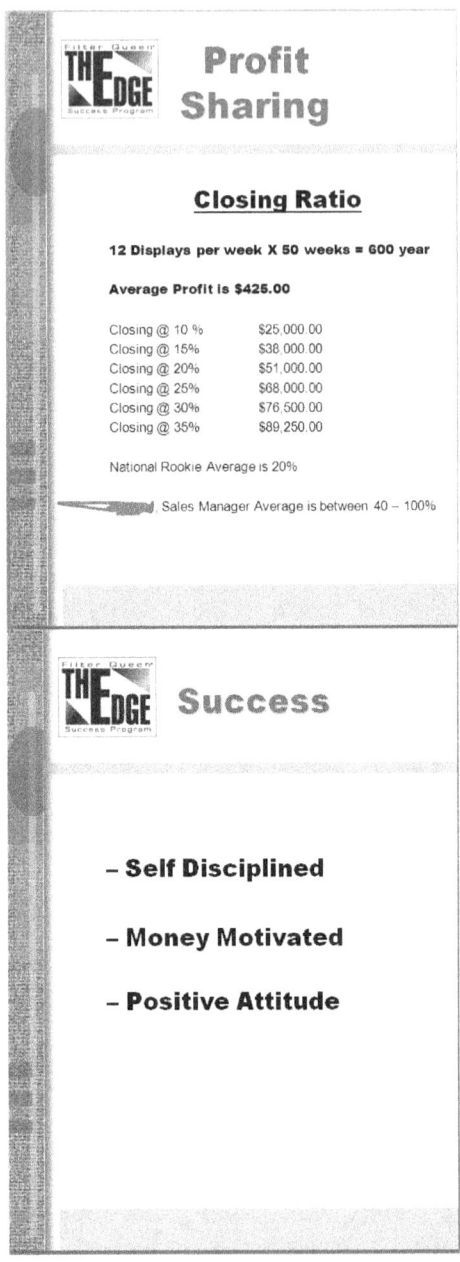

So after your interview where they show you this Class 2 medical device which the Defender, it removes dust particulate matter from the air. They tell you they fax your resume to head office (who faxes this day) and reply back in a period of time usually 24 hours,. Almost everyone who applies gets a call back with few exceptions.

SHOCK AND AWE PRESENTATION

The next day of the demonstration you get presented with a full product presentation, it is very well put together to sell the product with a lot of selling points covered and hooks thrown in.Then the close at the very end at the time it was $2599.00 for the vacuum "The Majestic" and 1299.00 for the air purifier the Defender. The biggest hook in my opinion was and is the cost of vacuums over the course of a life time. If you assume you go thru a $200 vacuum every 3 years that's 13 vacuums that blow dirt in your air. So not only are you paying to breathe dirt while you are wasting your time, Who would pick dirt up over here and throw it over there in their house right? Then there are the filters and why would you buy 14 vacuums when you can have 1 life time product that also cleans the air right or so I was sold. Then I sold others on the concept of the machine cleaning the air and surfaces while being a life long investment from a company that had been around since 1928. $2599 is not bad when you break the cost down over 20 years its $129.95 a year and if you're going thru "regular" vacuums at $200 a pop then you're out $4000 which is $ 1401 more than the filter queen cost what rational person would pay more for less service? You've already agreed at this point in the presentation as a witness that you wouldn't want your spouse to waste their time cleaning when the machine provided does not do the job and you agree you can't do the right job without the right tools. So when you are confronted with all the evidence your presented with the T close us vs them basically, the representative will close and say something like not bad eh and sit there and shut up till you say something, silence is a pressure tactic used there are many others but that's the final one and normally people will agree it's not a bad price for what they just saw over (2 hours). For a 15 minute presentation for a free gift to take their opinion on a medical device, the deception begins with the advertising sadly. Whether it's a flyer on your door indicating we have a package for you (tide or some other small gift like steak knives or a bbq set you know it's just another sales gimmick. I gave you something now you give me something and the only thing many want is to sell this machine. I believed I was helping people with their health and pocket book it was like a religious crusade against inferior machines and saving people money. Of course the carrot at the end of the 5 step program was your own office the idea others would be doing what you are now doing and you make more money because you have people selling for you and it's a numbers game. Meaning the more demos you do the more sales you will achieve, and they will get you doing 2 a day 3 at the least and they can be quite far from the initial agreement of a small radius around your home. Well maybe for some it materializes but not for me I completed the program had a meeting with my distributor and the president of the company in Canada his uncle and they rejected my achievements and at that point I was so discouraged and despaired, I had enough after a moment of reflection for the 3rd and final time.

After the demonstration day a percentage of people don't show up or return calls (I wish I had been one). You let them go and focus on the ones who show up out of desperation or duty whatever hooked them during the presentation, perhaps the idea of being your own boss is appealing as is helping others.

Those who stay after training are given the following form to fill out

INDEPENDENT CONTRACTOR AGREEMENT

CONTRACT FOR THE PROVISION OF DISTRIBUTION SERVICES

CONTRACT made this _____ day of _____ 20 ___

BETWEEN _____

(Hereafter referred to in the agreement as the Company)

AND _____

(Hereafter referred to in this agreement as the Contractor)

WHEREBY it is agreed as follows:

a) The Company has decided to engage the Contractor for the provision of certain services to it:

And

b) The Contractor has agreed to provide these services under the terms and conditions set out in this contract.

1. THE CONTRACT

This Contract is a contract for services between the Company. and _____

for the provision of distribution services associated with the promotion and sale of Filter Queen Products.

page 1 of 2

2. DISTRIBUTION SERVICES

2.1) Distribution services as referred to in this contract are distribution services by the Contractor for the Company of Filter Queen Products by way of in-home demonstrations and direct sale to end-users including all associated activities.

2.2) The Contractor is free to call on prospective customers at times and in areas as convenient to the Contractor.

2.3) The Contractor is responsible for the correct completion of all documents and paperwork as required by
   the Company relating to all services completed by the Contractor in clause 2.1.

2.4) The Contractor is responsible for all costs and

expenses associated with performing services as outlined in 2.1 and will receive no reimbursement of any costs by the Company

3. THE RELATIONSHIP BETWEEN THE CONTRACTOR AND THE COMPANY.

3.1)   The relationship between the Company and the Contractor is and shall be for all intents and purposes that of an Independent Contractor and neither this contract nor anything herein contained or implied shall constitute the relationship of Employer and Employee between the parties. For the avoidance of doubt, the parties acknowledge and agree that this Contract shall not operate as, or constitute an offer and/or contract of employment either during it's currency or expiry for whatever reasons.

4.   **REMUNERATION**

Remuneration from Sales of Filter Queen products. For each complete paid on sale, the Contractor will receive the following commissions:

System: $850 minus any discounts and banking fees.

Majestic: $525 minus any discount and banking fees.

Defender: $225 minus any discounts and banking fees.

Example: System sold at $3398 by cheque would be $850 Commission.

System sold at $3398 by Visa would be $792.40

System sold at $3398 by Desjardins (Regular finance) would be $816.40

4.1.2　　The company agrees to pay a Draw against commission for each complete demonstration performed by the contractor. Payment shall be equal to $40 per complete demonstration. A Complete demonstration constitutes the contractor contacting the office before commencing demonstration and again during the closing sequence from the customer home phone.

4.1.3　Payment will be calculated weekly with a work week beginning on Monday and ending on Sunday. Pay days are each Monday with one week being held back.

Both parties have read and agree to the terms of this contractor agreement.

Signed in the city of Saint John on _____ day of _____ 20_____

_____

_____

Print Name:　　　　Print Name:

Contractor　　　　　Distributor

WELCOME LETTER FROM THE PARENT COMPANY

HEALTH-MOR
An HMI Industries Inc. Company

Tuesday, April 17, 2007

Dear Adam Ness,

Congratulations on the start of your new career! We at Health-Mor would like to welcome you to the FILTERQUEEN Opportunity! We look forward to working with you at every level of the Edge Success Program, starting with your Distributor Dominic El-Tahhan, and your Executive Sales Staff Member for the FQ Quebec Division. Health-Mor created the Edge Success Program as a road map to guide you in your career with FILTERQUEEN. Through your hard work and commitment, you will discover all the benefits that the Edge Success Program has to offer in providing continuing education and wealth-building equity.

By now you should have received your square Enrollment Pin, a Passport to Success with the initial stamp, and your round IAQS Associate Pin from Dominic El-Tahhan. Health-Mor will send your Apprentice Certificate to your Promoting Distributor upon completion of your first two (2) warranted Unit sales.

Setting goals in your new career is important! Along with this letter we have included an IAQS Associate Monthly Goal Worksheet to help you set your personal budget and create a plan for what you will need to do to make your goals a reality! One of the foundations for success is education, and with the Edge Success Program you have the opportunity to take advantage of our many advanced training seminars. Within the first 2-3 weeks as an Apprentice, you should attend the 4-6 hour Jump Start seminar conducted by Healthy Living Home Ltd. This must be completed in order to advance to the next level of the Edge Program.

The FILTERQUEEN website is another great resource for new Associates. Not only will it allow you to manage your success and monitor your progress on the Edge Program, but you can also use it to keep up with the latest FILTERQUEEN news, contest standings and other exciting information! There is also a link to a health insurance provider if you and your family are in need of insurance. To access all of this information, simply go to www.filterqueen.com. At the bottom right of the home page, you will find the "Associate Login". Your username is your Social Security number and the password is your last name. If you have any issues accessing the website, please contact your Promoting Distributor.

We would also like to be able to communicate with you directly about upcoming events and other FILTERQUEEN news, so please let us know your email address upon receipt of this letter. You can send it to Michele Hall via email at mhall@filterqueen.com, or fax it to (440) 846-7900. Thank you for your cooperation. There is no limit to your success with FILTERQUEEN, and together we all succeed!

Sincerely,

The Health-Mor Sales Team

HEALTH-MOR WORLD HEADQUARTERS: 13325 Darice Parkway, Unit A • Strongsville, Ohio 44149 USA
Phone: 440-846-7800 • 1-800-760-4644 • Fax: 440-846-7899 • www.filterqueen.com

TRIAL BUY VACUUM

PASSPORT TO SUCCESS

TRIAL BUY VACUUM

Direct Selling Association
Code of Ethics for Sales

As an IAQS Associate you will:

- *Tell your customer who you are and what products you are selling.*
- *Explain how to return a product or cancel an order.*
- *Respect the customer's privacy by calling at a time that is convenient for them.*
- *Promptly end a demonstration or presentation at the customer's request.*
- *Provide accurate and truthful information regarding the price, quality, quantity, performance, and availability of the product.*
- *Offer a written receipt in a language the customer can understand.*
- *Provide contact information, as well as the contact information of the company you represent.*
- *Offer a complete description of any warranty or guarantee plan.*

I have read and understand the above.

IAQS Associate Signature: *(signed)*

Date: March /01 /2007

Official EDGE Participant

Name: Adam Mess
Office: Healthy Living Home Ltd.
Phone: (506) 458-9390

Code of issuing: Filter Queen
Passport No.: 255501490°

UNITED STATES DIVISION
FILTER QUEEN® OF THE AMERICAS

The Edge Success Program

LEVEL 1: Indoor Air Quality System Recruit

To be recognized as an IAQS Apprentice, you must:

- ☑ Complete the Distributor's initial training course.
- ☑ Sell one System or two Units.
- ☑ Submit Edge Enrollment Form and warranty names to your Distributor.

Level 1

Upon your recognition as an IAQS Apprentice, you will receive:

- An Apprentice Certificate
- The Edge Success Program Lapel Pin
- A stamp in your Associate Passport to Success

Healthy Living Home Ltd.
572 New Maryland Hwy.
New Maryland, NB.
E3C 1K1

Distributor Signature: *(signed)*

Date: _____

Congratulations, you are now an
IAQS Apprentice!

ADAM NESS

The Edge Success Program

LEVEL 2: IAQS Apprentice
To be recognized as an IAQS Technician, you must:

- ☑ OPTION 1 = Sell seven Systems (or 14 Units) per calendar month for two calendar months,
  or
  OPTION 2 = Sell 10 Systems (or 20 Units) in a calendar month.
- ☐ Attend a Jump Start Seminar.

Level 2

Upon your recognition as an IAQS Technician, you will receive:

- Two IAQS Vouchers for Unit sales
- A Jump Start Seminar Certificate
- A Technician Certificate
- A Technician Lapel Pin
- A stamp in your Associate Passport to Success

Healthy Living Home Ltd.
572 New Maryland Hwy.
New Maryland, NB.
E3C 1K1

Distributor Signature: _(signed)_

Date: _____

Congratulations, you are now an
IAQS Technician!

The Edge Success Program

LEVEL 3: IAQS Technician
To be recognized as an IAQS Senior Technician, you must:

- ☐ OPTION 1 = Sell seven Systems (or 14 Units) per calendar month for two calendar months,
  or
  OPTION 2 = Sell 10 Systems (or 20 Units) in a calendar month.
- ☐ Attend a Top Gun Seminar.

Level 3

Upon your recognition as an IAQS Senior Technician, you will receive:

- Two IAQS Vouchers for Unit sales
- A Top Gun Seminar Certificate
- One IAQS Voucher for completing a Top Gun Seminar
- A Senior Technician Certificate
- A Senior Technician Lapel Pin tab
- A stamp in your Associate Passport to Success

Healthy Living Home Ltd.
572 New Maryland Hwy.
New Maryland, NB.
E3C 1K1

Distributor Signature: _(signed)_

Date: _____

Congratulations, you are now an
IAQS Senior Technician!

TRIAL BUY VACUUM

The Edge Success Program
LEVEL 4: IAQS Senior Technician
To be recognized as an IAQS Specialist, you must:

- ☐ OPTION 1 = Sell seven Systems (or 14 Units) per calendar month for two calendar months,
  or
  OPTION 2 = Sell 10 Systems (or 20 Units) in a calendar month.
- ☐ Attend a Train the Trainer Seminar.

Level 4
Upon your recognition as an IAQS Specialist, you will receive:

- Two IAQS Vouchers for Unit sales
- A Train the Trainer Seminar Certificate
- One IAQS Voucher for completing a Train the Trainer Seminar
- A Specialist Certificate
- A Specialist Lapel Pin tab
- A stamp in your Associate Passport to Success

**Healthy Living Home Ltd.
572 New Maryland Hwy.
New Maryland, NB.
E3C 1K1**

Distributor Signature: _____

Date: _____

**Congratulations, you are now an
IAQS Specialist!**

The Edge Success Program
LEVEL 5: IAQS Specialist
To be recognized as a Candidate Regional Distributor, you must:

- ☑ Conduct interviews and four Associate training classes approved by Health-Mor.
- ☑ Submit training reports to your Master Distributor and Health-Mor.
- ☐ Redeem your eight IAQS Vouchers from Health-Mor.
- ☐ Sell eight Systems and establish a Distributor Equity Account with your sponsoring Master Distributor; funds to be used to open distributorship.
- ☐ Open personal savings account with your sponsoring Master Distributor to establish additional funds toward distributorship.

Level 5
Upon your recognition as an Candidate Regional Distributor, you will receive:

- Two IAQS Vouchers for completing training classes
- A Candidate Regional Distributor Certificate
- A Candidate Regional Distributor Lapel Pin tab
- A stamp in your Associate Passport to Success

Distributor Signature: _____

Date: _____

**Congratulations, you are now a
Candidate Regional Distributor!**

The Edge Success Program
LEVEL 6: Candidate Regional Distributor
To be recognized as a Regional Distributor, you must:

- ☐ Participate in the Financial Management Program with your sponsoring Master Distributor.
- ☐ Attend and complete a Pre-BMI workshop.
- ☐ Attend and graduate BMI at Eckerd College.
- ☐ Submit your Business Plan, including financial statements.
- ☐ Receive location approval from Health-Mor and your sponsoring Master Distributor.
- ☐ Submit Regional Distributor Agreement and proof of insurance to your sponsoring Master Distributor.

Level 6
Upon your recognition as a Regional Distributor, you will receive:

- One IAQS Voucher for completion of Pre-BMI
- Qualify for "Buy 10 Systems, Get Five Free" Program
- A Distributor Start-Up Kit
- Five Demonstration Kits
- A Regional Distributor Certificate
- A Regional Distributor Lapel Pin
- A Distributor Passport to Success with one stamp

Distributor Signature: _____

Date: _____

**Congratulations, you are now a
Regional Distributor!**

The Edge Success Program

The Goal of the Edge Success Program

The goal of the Edge Success Program is to help Associates develop their careers and businesses. The success of the individual within our Filter Queen® network is the key to the success of our entire organization. This exciting and exclusive program has been designed to reward Associates for their efforts and performance, guiding them step by step on a journey to success.

DEFINITIONS:

IAQS = Indoor Air Quality System, *the Filter Queen® Majestic® and Defender® sold together as a complete air quality system*

Unit = A Filter Queen Majestic® or Defender® sold individually

IAQS Associate = A general title for an independent salesperson (according to the Edge Success Program, levels one through five)

Rules & Regulations

The Recruiting for Success Program

IAQS Associates will:
1. Sponsor a new Recruit.
2. When a sponsored Recruit achieves Technician status, the sponsoring Associate will receive one "Recruiting for Success" IAQS Voucher.

- *No more than one IAQS Voucher can be earned per new Recruit.*
- *"Recruiting for Success" IAQS Vouchers are awarded in addition to the IAQS Vouchers in the Edge Program.*
- *IAQS Vouchers can only be redeemed upon becoming a Regional Distributor.*
- *There is no limit on the number of Edge "Recruiting for Success" IAQS Vouchers a sponsoring Associate can earn.*

IAQS VOUCHERS:
- *IAQS Vouchers have no cash value and expire after 24 months.*
- *Eight IAQS System Vouchers will be redeemed as part of the Equity Plan. All remaining IAQS Vouchers will be redeemed when (1) all the requirements for Regional Distributor status have been completed, (2) you have signed a Distributor Agreement with your sponsoring Master Distributor, and (3) you have signed a lease for your place of business.*

The Edge Success Program

Pin & Certificate Program

The Edge Success Pin and Certificate Program recognizes Associate achievement at each level of the program. The sponsoring Master Distributor is responsible for providing Associates with the appropriate pin, while Health-Mor provides the certificate.

LEVEL 1: *Upon completion, the sponsoring Master Distributor will award the Apprentice with the Edge Success Lapel Pin and Health-Mor Certificate of Achievement.*

LEVEL 2: *Upon completion, the sponsoring Master Distributor will award the Associate with the Edge Success Technician Lapel Pin and Health-Mor Certificate of Achievement.*

LEVEL 3: *Upon completion, the sponsoring Master Distributor will award the Associate with the Edge Success Senior Technician Lapel Pin tab and Health-Mor Certificate of Achievement.*

LEVEL 4: *Upon completion, the sponsoring Master Distributor will award the Associate with the Edge Success Specialist Lapel Pin tab and Health-Mor Certificate of Achievement.*

Rules & Regulations

LEVEL 5: *Upon completion, the sponsoring Master Distributor will award the Associate with the Edge Success Candidate Regional Distributor Lapel Pin tab and Health-Mor Certificate of Achievement.*

LEVEL 6: *Upon completion, the sponsoring Master Distributor will award the new Distributor with the Edge Success Regional Distributor Lapel Pin tab and Health-Mor Certificate of Achievement.*

The Edge Success Program

Distributor Equity Plan

When an Associate qualifies to be a Specialist and has conducted four training classes, he/she may redeem eight IAQS Vouchers for Systems to sell. The funds from those System sales are to be placed into an Equity Account with the sponsoring Master Distributor for his/her future business.

- *From each sale, the Associate will receive a cost of living commission (not to exceed present sales commission) and the sponsoring Distributor will receive a $200 operation fee. The remaining amount will be placed into an Equity Account.*

- *The Equity Account is the sponsoring Master Distributor's responsibility to establish.*

- *In the event the Candidate Distributor does not open within 120 days after graduating BMI, the sponsoring Master Distributor will be responsible for paying Health-Mor the prevailing Master Distributor price for the eight Systems. All remaining funds are to be dispersed to sponsoring Master Distributors.*

Rules & Regulations

Seminars

Jump Start Seminar: *A six-hour seminar that reviews the basics of the product display with new Associates, including: attitude, dress, referrals, and advanced hands-on role play.*

Top Gun Seminar: *A two-and-a-half-day seminar that takes the Associate to the Senior Technician level. It increases product display knowledge with a step-by-step analysis and "Ring of Fire." Top Gun examines the most effective lead programs, including customer book and referrals.*

Train the Trainer Seminar: *A three-day seminar that teaches Associates training principles. Train the Trainer covers ad planning and placement, the interview process, step-by-step training procedures, and follow-up schedules as well as other training topics.*

The Edge Success Program

The BMI Experience

The Business Management Institute is designed to prepare the Candidate Regional Distributor for the challenges that all new business owners experience. There are three phases to the completion of the BMI Experience.

PHASE 1: The Eckerd College Package *When a Candidate Regional Distributor registers for BMI, Eckerd College mails an information package that includes a correspondence course and personality tests. The correspondence course is the first step in creating a business plan, to be developed in Pre-BMI. The personality tests are an important part of the BMI experience and should be sent back to Eckerd immediately.*

PHASE 2: Pre-BMI *All Candidate Regional Distributors must attend a Pre-BMI workshop with Health-Mor's Director of Distributor Development or other Health-Mor designated trainer. This important workshop looks at the Distributor checklist and budgets used to develop a business plan to successfully open a Filter Queen® Distributorship and sets the stage for the fast pace of BMI. Health-Mor will send the Candidate Regional Distributor one IAQS Voucher to offset the cost of attending BMI.*

Rules & Regulations

PHASE 3: BMI *This five-and-a-half day program includes the following topics: (1) financial management, (2) leadership development, (3) legal and ethical issues, (4) business plan development, and (5) marketing and training methods. BMI is held at Eckerd College, St. Petersburg, Florida, three times a year. A Distributor may not open an office until they have completed the BMI Experience.*

IMPORTANT: *In no way does the Edge Success Program create a contractual agreement between Health-Mor and an Associate or Distributor.*

ADAM NESS

The Edge Success Program
Sales Log

The following pages have been provided to help you track your sales for the next year. Check one box for each Unit sale and two for each System sale.

Month _____ Year _____

1	2	3	4	5	6	7	8	9	10	11
12	13	14	15	16	17	18	19	20	21	22
23	24	25	26	27	28	29	30	31		

Month _____ Year _____

1	2	3	4	5	6	7	8	9	10	11
12	13	14	15	16	17	18	19	20	21	22
23	24	25	26	27	28	29	30	31		

Sales Log

Month _____ Year _____

1	2	3	4	5	6	7	8	9	10	11
12	13	14	15	16	17	18	19	20	21	22
23	24	25	26	27	28	29	30	31		

Month _____ Year _____

1	2	3	4	5	6	7	8	9	10	11
12	13	14	15	16	17	18	19	20	21	22
23	24	25	26	27	28	29	30	31		

Autographs / Notes

Part# 2 555 0149 00 Rev. A 1/01

MY TRAINING

My first demo I seen was a shock and awe presentation preformed by one masterful performer entertainer Jesus piece wearing self proclaimed religious family man. Who in the end was more money motivated than anything else or that would become my assessment later on. He was selling the dream and the machine, you are essentially taught you're waging war on dirt and who doesn't think having a clean and healthy home is a good idea? Who thinks breathing in dirt is good? Or who likes to spend more on inferior products then a superior one for less than the lifetime cost of those inferior products? During my Training a red flag went up he responded to someone's tax question with (CRA they have no right to take that money from you it's yours you earned it) I knew he was wrong but he was also new to the country I was told. Also his English was not the best at the time he was still making mistakes, so I chalked it up to that and he went made people feel small and insignificant if questioned so I didn't want any public shaming it should have been enough to tell me to get out. I was sold on the idea of a family oriented business that earned a decent income while helping people out. This was a crusade against dirt and dirty machines. And he had already gone over the Edge program stating no one can hold you back you make your own success with this, to me that was a no barrier way to get my own office and train people to be professional sales persons,. I had some training and coaching experience with others from Connect North America on various products. I was sold on him being a genuine decent human being who cared about people's health from a war torn country Lebanon who was living at his in-laws place. (where I would pick him up more than once) He lived there while he was renting out his house to 2 other sales associates what a nice guy or so I thought.

SOME PRACTICE DEMOS I DID

The first demo I did was for my mother who I knew was not interesting in purchasing a filter queen, again as she and my father had purchased one before. She went thru the motions and pretended to be a customer and I was the sales rep as it was the first time I was doing the presentation I wanted familiarity. I had sales experience before but not person to person directly in your face. So after the presentation I did my Trading call as required to the office and they were not too hard on me this first time ,though they did try and phone sell my mom who said no thank you have a nice day and hung up.

Another demo I did was for my mom's work friend Sandra as this was my first non known contact presentation, mom came along for the ride also it was her friend and she did not want a lot of pressure put on her by myself after seeing the demo or by the office. Sandra informed me she was interested in the air purifier at the end of the presentation and then mom talked her out of it and I did not interject as it would have started a awkward situation, and I was content for the morale boost of doing this presentation in front of someone I barely knew.

Yet another presentation I did knowing it would not be a sale was for my father and his lady at his place we went thru the presentation they replied to the questions as normal people do. Then they informed me they would not be purchasing a filter queen this was a foregone conclusion again I was out for practice and I was content with my achievements.

I did sell on my practice demos, the next one was to one of my best buddies who would end up helping me move stuff from our house before we moved later on to Bathurst. Brad and his wife at the time had decided to purchase a full combo the vacuum and air purifier both. Sadly for them and me they were declined. But I filled out my first contract that day and that was new and an accomplishment that I would repeat many more times.

My final practice demos were 2 defender sales one a piece one to Joe and his wife and one to David. Joe was a former work college of mine and David was a friend from grade 3 in school. Joe bought on approved financing which let me fill out another contract for that application and David bought with a credit card meaning I got paid that week no fuss it was around a $500 cheque and where I was still doing hours at the call center it worked well and that is like hitting the jackpot on a lotto machine for motivation to keep going.

MARKETING PART
1 CLIENTS

It is not possible to calculate how many numerous hours my wife and I folded bingo flyers in our home on unpaid time. These flyers would be mailed out and every flyer was a winner. Unfortunately I found out later my distributor did not mail out the TV or BBQ winning flyers. So all people won was tide or steak knives, 10$ cab fare, or a pizza voucher for 10$ off. That was one method another was driving around placing sticky notes on mail boxes or on doors indicating there was package being held for you and to call this number.

Bingo flyers

TELE-NOTICE
MASTER CHART

225 - 1000	B	23 61 16	JUG OF TIDE OR 12 STEAK KNIVES
250 - 1000	I	2 19 20	$50.00 GAS CARD OR $50.00 GROCERY CARD
3 - 1000	N	88 48 32	COLOR T.V. OR BBQ
294 - 1000	G	11 27 52	7 PIECE CARVING KNIVES WITH CUTTING BOARD
225 - 1000	O	31 14 81	DELUX STAINLESS STEEL BBQ SET OR 6 PIECE STEAK KNIVES WITH WOOD BLOCK

Of course when not answering incoming calls the folks in the telemarketing department are busy placing calls like this;

Good morning/aft/eve, how are you today? You don't know me, my name is_____. I'm calling form Healthy Living Home in Fredericton and we are conducting a simple six question survey and I'm hoping you can take 30 seconds to help me?

1) Does any member of your family have asthma or allergies?
2) Are there any smokers in your household?
3) Do you have an air exchanger or air purifier or both?
4) Do you live in an apartment, house or duplex?
5) Do you think the air quality is worst indoor or outdoor?
6) What age group are you in? 21-40,

41-55, 56-70 or other?

7) Since a lot of breathing problems are work related may I ask what type of work you do? And your husband/wife?

Thank you very much for helping our company with our survey and for doing so, you will be registered for random daily drawings of a selection of great gifts, if your phone number is drawn, who should we ask for? _____(bob), and your last name Bob? _____

Thanks again and have a great day!

The objective is to make a list of people to contact for demonstrations and qualify them, for to potential approvals as in cash or credit. The following scripts were used in the Fredericton office.

DIRECT CALL

Hello! May I speak to the lady of the house please? My Name is _____, you don't know me, I'm calling from Healthy Living Home in Fredericton and the reason I am calling is we're doing some advertising and we're giving people a jug of tide for their help. Do you use tide?

If Yes Great! Proceed to book (alternate of Choice)

Upon booking, explain the guy that delivers gets paid $20 for displaying the Defender and Majestic etc….

"What are the products?" explain and proceed to book

(ALTERNATE OF CHOICE)

"How long does it take?" Say 35 minutes or so, depending on how many questions they ask. (Proceed to book with alternate of choice)

"I'm not interested" There is no interest required, you still get a jug of tide and the guy still gets paid for his time to show you the products. (Proceed to book with alternate of choice)

THE LIES

The sales rep does not get paid 20$ for their time in the first few weeks they "guarantee" you will be paid but there was a week or more where, I had no sales and was not paid the $200 or so for the week meaning I had to use savings to pay for my employment gas while other bills accumulated and they keep telling the prospects you are paid for this time, this is to 'remove 'the pressure the demo will put on them.

I remember a time I was placing calls being more honest then my Jesus piece wearing boss would have liked. He asked me do you want to sell the demo or the tide on the phone as I was talking up the products and I did not answer in a way he liked. He indicated the tide was an easier sell on the phone. It really sucked being called down for being a honest decent person reconcile that with being a boy scout and ardent believer of the faith of that movement for a long time.

MARKETING PART 2
HIRING SALES PEOPLE

You think they treat the customers pretty bad off the hop with the dishonest approach it's not any better for in house recruiting of local talent. Here are some ads placed in the Greater Fredericton Area after I was employed there.

HIRING ADS PICTURES

These ads are placed on the internet in classifieds or in news papers. They work because people see the money then at the slick interview they are impressed by a class 2 medical device and the slide show. Which shows income and they say something like you can do better than 10% closing cant you, if you agree to this you assume you'll be getting 25000$ good luck. They don't mention at all that there is an approval ratio and some or a fair number of your sales will be declined and you are not paid for those.

Kijiji Fredericton > jobs > sales, retail sales > Ad ID 168174890

⭐ **Professional Career**

Date Listed	11-Nov-09
Address	Canada

Big Opportunity available in the East of Canada. Starting in the Fredericton office, a professional training seminar will be conducted to qualify 6 representatives to service our customers localy & around NB.
Email Resume : himit@nb.aibn.com

Visits: 299

ADAM NESS

Kijiji Fredericton > jobs > sales, retail sales > Ad ID 168642509

Positivity is our power! Come join our great team!

Date Listed   15-Nov-09
Address   Canada

AAA-1 OPPORTUNITY $20.00/Hr Base Agreement
$500.00 SIGNING BONUS.Large electrical manufacturers Distributor expanding In the Fredericton area and needs8-10 full-time men & women for various positions includingCustomer service.NO EXPERIENCE NECESSARY.Operators on duty Call (506)458-2393 Sat 9-5, Mon 9-5 ,Tue 9-5

Visits: 694

Kijiji Fredericton > jobs > part time, students > Ad ID 168638506

Set your own schedule.

Date Listed   13-Nov-09
Address   Canada

Students start part time now and full time when school lets out.Duties are delivering and explaining small electrical equipment. Car required .
Call (506)458-2393 Ask for Mr Tahhan, or Email you resume to   dt@nb.aibn.com.

Visits: 178

Kijiji Fredericton > jobs > customer service > Ad ID 168162636

Customer Service

Date Listed   11-Nov-09
Address   ▬▬▬ St, Fredericton, NB, Canada
               View map

Local branch of International Company needs people in several departments.Customer Service,Delivery & Assembly,& Services.No exp.Nec.Big opportunity.
If you can start tuesday Nov/17/2009,Email your resume to hlh@nb.aibn.com

Visits: 592

TRAINING THE DEMO AND PRACTICE DEMOS

The following text is what they will get you to memorize and parrot back and then 'practice' on your friends, it's also a way to market products, get your friends who trust you to see you doing a demonstration who you gave a free gift to too. They want to help you so maybe they feel obligated to purchase or they like the product or both. Before you go you'll do it in the office a bunch of times in front of a person or persons.

Here are a couple pieces of paper they hand out to help you control the presentation

INTANGIBLES OF THE DEMO

1) Door Entry – always have a firm handshake
2) Setting the stage – have husband and wife sit together on the sofa,

MOVE COFFEE TABLE, TURN TV OFF.

3) No more than 3 feet from Customer
4) Get on first name basis
5) Plug machine and lamp into separate sockets
6) Always be kneeling when doing demo, people do not like to feel intimidated by people standing over them.
7) Eye Contact
8) Always leave booklet open at customers feet
9) Tone of Voice
10) Always refer back to booklet
11) Attachment case never left
12) Place test pads in two neat line at customers feet
13) Always hold lamp straight down at eye level for customer to get the full effect of what's going back into the air.
14) Make sure you ask questions (Get customers involved)
15) Keep lamp on for 5 – 10 seconds to show

what is going back into their home.

16) Always get the customers vacuum out and get them to admit that they do not want to use it anymore.

"Bob, if you came home and Mary was using the vacuum and you saw all this dust coming out the exhaust, what would you think"? (She's wasting her time!) "Mary, now that you know that you're wasting your time using this machine, do you want to keep using it"? (No!) "Bob, do you want her to keep using it"? (No) Folk's you're going to love your new Filter Queen, you're just going to love it!

17) Have customer try the Filter Queen at least 4 times during the demonstration.
18) Always use alternate choice questions when closing.
19) Should be taught persistence for customer to make a decision.
20) Should be taught proper phone close.
21) Importance of Clean Equipment
22) Bring back boxes and trade-in from every sale.
23) How to get referrals
24) Post selling. Make sure customer knows how to use their machine

25) How to fill out contracts properly
26) Taught how to tear apart as many vacuums as possible.

THE 2 HOUR DEMO YOU WERE TOLD WOULD BE LESS THAN 35 MINUTES

Buying Questions are any question someone would ask them selves before they purchase something. For example, before you would purchase a new car. You would ask yourself am I looking for a luxury car, a sports car, or an economy car? Do I want a 2 door or a 4 door? An automatic or a stick shift? Bucket or bench seats? Leather or cloth seats? What type of guarantee does it have? These are some of the questions some one would ask them selves before they purchase a car. If you were going to sell a professional buyer, your presentation would be 15 minutes long and for the next hour all they would do is ask you questions and if you got them all right, they would buy it from you. Buying questions consist of 2 formulas the first is **Feature Advantage and Benefit**, this is anytime your talking about the features of the Filter Queen itself. The following are buying questions using the **FAB FORMULA.**

The Base: Most machines have 3 wheels, one in the front, two in the back or two in the front and one in the back. They tip over a lot and they are hard to pull around corners. That is why Filter Queen has 4 wheels, they are riveted on, so they will never come off and it has a rubber bumper so it will protect your furniture.

The Hose: Most hoses are 3 to 5 feet long, they are never long enough to get at the hard to reach at places and they tend to keep tipping the machines over. Your Filter Queen hose is 8 feet long so you can reach wherever you like. Another problem they found with most hoses, is from going around corners, they tend to clog and lose power. Your Filter Queen hose is neoprene rubber reinforced with piano wire, which is one of the strongest wires in the world, so you'll never have that problem. Most hoses tend to split and crack around the ends; with your Filter Queen you'll never have that problem because there are 360 degree swivel ends so there is never any tension on the hose.

The Bucket: If you were to pick these bullets up with a bag type system, what do you think would happen?

(Break the motor) With your Filter Queen you'll never have that problem because the metal deflector deflects everything to the side and the bottom, never allowing anything to touch the motor. The bucket is made of ABS PLASTIC, which is the same material that Hockey and Football helmets are made of. Most vacuums, you have to change the bag every week to two weeks because they only hold 2 pints of dirt. Your

Filter Queen holds 2 1/2 gallons of dirt, which is 5x more than a regular bag, which will save you a lot of money on bags, wouldn't it?

The Motor: Most vacuum use a ¼ hp motor, the more expensive ones use a ½ hp motor. They're not powerful enough to get the deep down dirt. That is why Filter Queen has designed for you a 1.22 hp motor, which is the most powerful motor on the market today.

The Crown: With most vacuums, your tools are stored in the closet. Now Mary if you were doing the cleaning on a Saturday and you needed a tool for the corner there and it was upstairs in the closet, what would you do? (I'll do it next time) And you know the old saying "Next time never comes" does it? (NO) That is why Filter Queen has designed for you the crown. The crown hold all the tools right on top saving you a lot of time and effort and when you get those cleaning results, you'll start cleaning with a pleasure right? (Right)

Curtain and Upholstery Tool: Most vacuums curtain and upholstery tool have no brush therefore there is no airflow and it is hard on your furniture. The filter Queen has added a brush which allows airflow therefore when you clean your curtains you get the dirt and not the curtain. It is also very soft on your furniture and the brush loosens the dirt and allows the FQ to pick it up.

Dusting Brush: Most dusting brushes are

made of nylon or plastic, which scratches your fine furniture. The Filter Queen dusting brush is made of soft horsehair, which allows you to clean your fine furniture with complete confidence you're protecting them.

Crack and Crevice Tool: Most crevice tools are soft so when you go down the side of sofas it closes up which means you're working for nothing. Your Filter Queen Crevice tool is made of the same material plumbers pipes are made of, so it will never close up and allow you to get all the dirt.

Magic Wand: Most wands are made of either Plastic or chrome plated steel. If they are plastic, they tend to crack and lose power. If they are made of chrome plated steel and there is any humidity they tend to rust together and you can't take them apart. Your Filter Queen wand is made of Stainless Steel so it will never rust and the ends have a rubber to metal connection so it will never lose power.

Floor Brush: Most floor brushes are all the same height, so they end up pushing the dirt forward instead of picking it up. The Filter Queen floor brush is made of horsehair so it is soft on your floors; the front brushes are cut so it allows you to suck the dirt up instead of pushing it forward.

Power-Nozzle: The Power-Nozzle has an extra 1/8hp motor, it has a soft rubber bumper so it will not leave any marks on walls and furniture, and it has a V-shaped brush, which pulls the dirt to the center where the most airflow is. It has a height adjuster for different types of carpet.

The Defender:

The Defender is made of Abs plastic and weighs only 10 lbs so it is portable.

It has a 3 speed motor which on low speed changes the air in a 10 X 10 room 2x an hour, on medium 6 times an hour and on high speed 12 time an hour.

The Defender Filter filters down to 0.1 micron, which is better than HEPA, the industry standard used in hospitals. Most air cleaner filters need to be changed every 3 months because they are small toy type filters, your Defender filter consists of over 40 square feet of material and lasts up to one year so it will save you a lot of money on filters. The Charcoal filter will filter out nearly 300 different gases and odours and last up to six months.

The Defender uses .8 amps on low speed and 1.8 amps on high speed, which is less electricity than two 100-watt bulbs. So it is very cheap on electricity.

Most air cleaners are square and they take the air in from only one direction, so you have to keep pointing to where you want to clean the air. Your Defender takes the air in from 360 degrees so it does not matter where you put it in the room.

Most air cleaners have a 90day warranty. The Defender has a 1yr guarantee on all parts and the motor, and as long as you change the filter each year it renews itself for an additional year for life.

The second Formula is Problem Solution Close. This formula is used anytime you are comparing what they are using now (A Bag type system) with the Filter Queen.

Vac Teardown: Bob if you came home from work and Mary was using the vacuum and you saw all this dirt coming out, what would you think? (Bob: She's wasting her time!) Mary, now that you know that you are wasting your time using this machine, do you want to keep using it? (Mary: No) Bob, do you want here to keep using it? (Bob: No) Folk's you're going to love your new Filter Queen, you're just going to love it!!

Clean Curtains: Us: Mary, how do you normally clean the curtains?

Mary: Take them down and wash them.

Us: You have to take them down, put them in the washer, put them in the dryer and then hang them back up. It's much easier with the Filter Queen. Can you see how it would save you a lot of laundry time and money?

Mary: Yes!

	Us:	(Show dirt) Now Bob this is not Mary's fault if you don't have the proper tool, you cannot get the proper job done can you?
	Bob:	No!
	Us:	At the same time Mary, do you ever sneeze (Poof) when you pass the vacuum?
	Mary:	Yes!
	Us:	That's the 19 – 43% we were talking about before that goes through your bag back into the air and you breathe all that dust in, do you think that it is good for your health?
	Mary:	No!
	Us:	So you can see how the Filter Queen would help to protect the health aspect in your home wouldn't it?
	Them:	Yes!
	Us:	At the same time where do you think all this dust is going to land?
	Them:	Back onto our furniture.
	Us:	So why waste your time picking it up.
Clean Top of Sofa: sofa do you?	Us:	Bob you don't walk on top of your
	Bob:	No!
	Us:	(Clean top of sofa) Bob, can you imagine coming home from work, taking a shower and then sitting on the sofa and putting your head in this? (Show dirt pad) Now again Bob, this is not Mary's fault. You're probably wandering how all this dirt got on

top of the sofa since no body walks or sits there. 95% of the dirt that comes into our home comes in on our clothes and shoes. The dirt ends up on the carpet and Mary comes by with your vacuum and all this dust (Poof) goes back into the air and you know the old saying: "What goes up must come down" and it doesn't pick and chose where it lands the dirt lands everywhere. So what was once a small pile on the carpet is now all over you living room.

Clean Bob's Cushion: Us: Bob, you don't like to sit on dirt do you?

Bob: Of course not!

Us: (clean cushion) Again Bob this is not Mary's fault because you have to remember the vacuum you're using at present does not have the power the Filter Queen has and I'm sure you'd agree you need that power to get the deep down dirt don't you?

Bob: Yes!

Us: However, even if you had the power, you'd still be tossing (Poof) all this dust back into the air and back onto your furniture. Now Bob, if I came into your home with a bag of dirt and I started tossing dirt all over your home, what would you do to me?

Bob: Kick you out!

Us: What do you think we should do with your old vacuum over there since it does it every time Mary turns it on?

Bob: Kick it out!

Clean T.V. Screen: Us: Folks, you don't let your children watch dirty movies do you?

Them: No!

Us: (Clean TV. and show dirt) look at that even if they were to watch Sesame street they would be watching a dirty movie. Now Bob, anyone coming in during the day can see the time and effort that Mary puts into cleaning the home, but besides all that we were still able to pick all this dirt up (Show dirt). Not because you're not cleaning the home Mary but, simply because the tools you're using at present are not doing the proper job are they?

Mary: No!

Us: At the same time if you were using a system with a bag inside you'd be tossing (Poof) all this dust back into the air and back onto your furniture. Now tell me folks, does it make sense to use a system that tosses dust back into the air?

Them: No!

Us: That is the same fine dust that the Filter Queen filter filters each and every time you use it. It will cut down on the cleaning of the home and at the same time give you a clean home.

Clean Stereo Speaker: Us: Tell me folks, did you ever notice static sometimes when you have the stereo on?

Them: Sometimes

Us: What that is, is fine dust on the speakers and with the vibration of the speaker it causes static. (Clean Speaker & Show dirt)

Folks, can you see how your new Filter Queen will help to protect the assets in your home?

Them: Yes!

Us: At the same time if we were using a system with a bag inside (Poof) again you'd be blowing all this dirt right back in to your air.

Clean Lamp Shade: Us: Folks did you ever notice that when you bought that lamp it was bright and

Ever since then it's not as bright. (Clean lampshade and show dirt) Once again you can see how the Filter Queen will give you the clean home you work so hard for. However, if you were to still continue to use a bag type system (Poof) you're just rearranging the dirt. Bob, trying to clean your home with a bag type vacuum is like trying to shovel sand with a pitchfork. Now Bob, if I gave you a pitchfork and told you to go shovel a hole in the sand, what would you say?

Bob: You're crazy!

Us: Isn't that the same thing as asking Mary to give you a clean home with a vacuum that blows dirt back into the air?

Clean Coffee table: Us: Folks, how do you normally do your dusting on your fine furniture?

Them: Pledge or Endust.

Us: Bob, when do you wax your car, before or after your clean it?

Bob: After, of course!

Us: Imagine for a moment, you have dust on the table. You wet it with wax and then you grind it into the table where it scratches and then you fill it in with wax? (Clean coffee table and show dirt) Look at all this dirt; can you imagine grinding that into your fine furniture?

Them: No!

Us: Again with a bag system you're still blowing all this dust back into the air. Can you see why your cleaning is never done?

Clean corner of Sofa: Us: (Clean corner of sofa and show dirt) Now Bob, this is not Mary's fault as we mentioned before you need the power to get the deep down dirt don't you?

Bob: Yes!

Us: Now I can't help but notice we picked up a lot of food from inside your sofa there. Now Bob, if I went out to your refrigerator and we unplugged it and left it alone for a month and at the end of the month, we opened it up, what would it be like in there?

Bob: Mold, mildew etc.

Us: What do you think is happening to this food inside your sofa?

Bob: Same thing

Us: Even worst because you come by with your vacuum and you (Poof) all these germs and bacteria back into the air for your family to breathe, you couldn't design a better system to destroy their health could you?

Them: No!

Us: At the same time those are the fine dust particles that your Filter Queen filter filters out every time for you, protecting your family's health.

Clean Baseboard: Us: Folks, you don't walk along your walls do you?

Them: No!

Us: (Clean baseboard and show dirt) Now folks, you're probably wandering why we pick up all this dirt a long your walls. You see this dirt was once in the middle of the floor again Mary came by with your old machine picked it up and (poof) blew it against the wall and it fell along the baseboards.

Clean with Wand: Us: Now Bob, this is not Mary's fault. You notice we pick up all this dirt from the hard to get at spots and you know the old saying: "If it's hard to get at, you just don't do it". So you can see how with her nice new Filter Queen you'll get a total cleaning of the home, right Mary?

Mary: Right!

Us: However, if she was forced to continue using a system with a bag inside, you might as well sit down and have a coffee because you're not cleaning any thing are you?

Them Right!

Clean Floor: Us: (Clean floor and show dirt) Wow! Look at all this dirt, again if you don't have the proper tool, you can't expect to get the proper job done can you?

Them: No!

Us: At the same time I hope Mary doesn't pass the vacuum (poof) at the same time you're eating, you're probably wandering where did all the pepper come from? I bet all this time you thought it was spices didn't you?

Comparison Test: Us: Folks, now do you believe me when I told you before that it is not Mary's fault but the fault of the system you are using at present?

Them   Yes!

Bread Test: Us: Bob and Mary, you see the fine dust on the filter here and on the inside of the bucket?

Them: Yes!

Us;   That's the fine dust you saw going through your vacuum before. That's is the fine dust that goes through a bag type system every time you use it. For example Bob, if you came home on a Monday night and you saw all this dust on your sofa there, what would you do?

Bob: Yell at Mary and have her pass the vacuum.

Us: But, see that's the fine dust that goes through the bag and Tuesday night you come home and see it there again. Pass the vacuum, Wednesday night the exact same thing. You see that's the fine dust you will never get rid of as long as you are using a system with a bag inside. At the same time you're breathing (poof) all this dust in, do you think that is good for your health?

Them: No

Us: So you can see how your new Filter Queen will help to protect the health aspect in your home wouldn't it?

Them: Yes!

Us: At the same time, if the vacuum you have at present were doing the proper job, do you think we would've be able to pick up all this dirt?

Them: No!

Us: So you can see how your new Filter Queen really is the answer to the dust and dirt problems in your home isn't it?

Them: Yes!

Us: Folks, this whole presentation boils down to 2 things. If the Filter Queen stays, all this dust, dirt and pollution goes. If the Filter Queen goes, all this dust dirt and pollution stays. Which would you rather live with the Filter Queen or the dirt?

Them: The Filter Queen.

THE CLOSE

NOW THE PRICE OF THE FILTER QUEEN IS JUST 2499, THE DEFENDER ROOM AIR CLEANER IS JUST $1199. NOT BAH EH!!

Now we accept Cash, Visa, Mastercard, Personal Cheque and we even have a Monthly Family investment plan. Which one of these would be most convenient for you?

Now folks these are what the prices are normally for anyone who calls us on the telephone or comes into our stores, these are what the prices are. They don't go up and they don't go down. However we called you, you didn't call us and it's an advertising promotion. Obviously, if you take one and your friends come in and see it, they will want one and they will be paying these prices here. However, we found that 99% of the people who see the Filter

Queen would rather be using a Filter Queen than what they are presently using. Mary, if you got up tomorrow morning and had to clean the house, you have the Filter Queen sitting here and your old vacuum over there, which one would you use? (THE FILTER QUEEN) So if you got a Filter Queen today, what would you do with your old machine? (Throw it out or sell it or give it to some one) Well because it's an advertising promotion for **TODAY AND TODAY ONLY WHILE I'M IN YOUR HOME THE COMPANY AUTHORIZES ME** to give you a $300 trade-in value for your old machine bringing the price of your Filter Queen to just $2199 and if you were taking it with the Defender because you're taking the complete system, I'm also authorized to give you a $200 discount on the Defender bringing the price of your Defender to just $999. Now with as little as $500 down I can place it in your home for just $500 per month. **How does that sound to you? **(WAIT FOR ANSWER)**

If answer is positive, write them up

If answer is negative, If it were affordable would you get one today? (YES) do T-close

4) Folks if you were to get the Filter Queen would you be taking it with or without the Defender. (With Defender Go to step 5. With out, go to step 5)

Bob and Mary, you've heard the problem that the food banks are having, they are on the news all the time? (YES) Well our company sponsors the Daily Bread Food Bank here in Moncton and to help you get the Filter Queen at a really good price and at the same time help the needy in our community. Again for **TONIGHT AND TONIGHT ONLY** the **COMPANY AUTHORIZES ME** to give you $20 off for every can or dry food item you give me to donate to the food bank up to a maximum of 10 items. You'd have no problem giving 10 items for the food bank would you? (NO) Great! So you be saving a total of $900 today bring the price of your Filter Queen to $1999 and with as $300 down I can place it in your home for just $150 a month. Now whose name would you like me to the warranty in? **(WAIT FOR ANSWER)**

If answer is positive, write them up

IF ANSWER IS NEGATIVE, DO T-CLOSE OR GO TO STEP 6

Bob and Mary between you and I what is the real reason you're not getting a Filter Queen tonight?

Call Office:

_____ I'm here at Bob and Mary's house and they are super nice people. I picked up a mountain of dirt but it's not their fault. They are trying to clean their beautiful home with a dirt leaking, dust blowing, germ polluting (Vacuum) . Now I've offered them the maximum I'm allowed to, however they feel _objection_ . Is there anything you can do to help these nice people out?

THE TRADING CALL

This was most unfunny of experiences I don't think I've been screamed at more in my life for being real I mean I sold a lot, but not every day and not every week. When you did not sell they would try to close you on closing your customer. The one I worked for could make you feel like you were lacking for not selling. Like you just spent 2 hours likely in this person's home to get their opinion on a class 2 medical device, for which if you had been with the company longer than a month you were not getting 20$ a hour as advertised to the prospect on the phone. I remember times when I was sent on a 100% French demo more than once and often I did sell them with my limited knowledge of French being superior to all other Anglophones at the company. One of those demos I made a mistake, my boss being from Lebanon and me knowing that was a French territory and I figured he'd have some knowledge of French, oops. I handed the customer the phone to talk to him after her credit was rejected, well she kind of let him have it fast and furious in 1 – 3 minutes, then she handed the phone back to me and he yelled so loud the customer could hear him. Thankfully she did not speak English so she did not have to bear witness to his rudeness.

On the wall is a poster like follows this most likely grabs your attention. Which funny now enough looking back was used as a justification to stay employed there " no one can hold you back" which is some of the biggest BS I was sold, by my distributor because he even lied to his uncle for the trip to Florida. Which I witnessed as he would take sales numbers from me and one other person and say another person sold them sure I still got paid my commission for my sale but it looked like the other persons had achieved something they had not. All in an effort to portray success for the distributor(s) at the filter queen convention.

THE EDGE SUCCESS POSTER

BEFORE YOU
HEAD OUT YOU
ARE GIVEN AN
INSTRUCTION SHEET
FOR YOUR TOILS

INSTRUCTION SHEET

DEAR TRAINEE,

AS YOU KNOW, IN ORDER TO BECOME PROFICIENT IN ANYTHING YOU MUST PRACTICE. YOU WERE ALSO TOLD WHEN HIRED THAT OUR COMPANY WOULD HELP SUPPLY APPOINTMENTS FOR YOU, WHICH IS OF COURSE CORRECT.

OUR LARGEST SINGLE EXPENSE IS THE APPOINTMENT PROCUREMENT; EACH INDIVIDUAL APPOINTMENT IS QUITE COSTLY. THEREFORE WE WANT YOU TO BE AS PROFICIENT AS POSSIBLE BEFORE YOU START ON OFFICE APPOINTMENTS. IN ORDER TO INCREASE CONFIDENCE AND PRODUCT KNOWLEDGE DURING YOUR DEMONSTRATION, WE HAVE INSTITUTED A POLICY FOR EACH TRAINEE TO PERFORM (10) PRACTICE DEMONSTRATIONS BEFORE THEY ARE ISSUED OFFICE APPOINTMENTS. THESE PRACTICE DEMONSTRATIONS SHOULD BE MADE WITH FRIENDS, RELATIVES, ACQUAINTANCES, ETC. THIS WILL ENABLE YOU TO DEMONSTRATE WITH CONFIDENCE AND ALLOW YOU TO FOCUS ON WHAT YOU'VE LEARNED OVER THE PAST 3 DAYS.

Below is a telephone approach to help you set up for your

practice weekend.

The reason I'm calling is that I just started a new position with a company called Healthy Living Home and before I get started I need to practice what I will be doing for them. I just need 60 minutes or so of your time so that I can come out and show you what I am doing for the company. It would be greatly appreciated! (And set a time for this weekend!!)

QUALIFICATIONS

1) IF MARRIED, BOTH MUST BE PRESENT TO WATCH DEMONSTRATION.

2) ALL PRACTICE DEMONSTRATIONS MUST BE GIVEN TO ADULTS, WHO IN TURN MUST BE *GAINFULLY EMPLOYED OR RETIRED*.

3) SCHEDULE APPOINTMENTS NO CLOSER THAN 2 HOURS APART.

4) DO NOT SCHEDULE ANY APPOINTMENTS BEFORE 5:00 PM ON FRIDAY.

5) CALL INTO THE OFFICE BEFORE LEAVING EACH PRACTICE APPOINTMENT.

6) MUST BE HOME OWNERS

Trainee's Name: _____   Trainee's Number (_____)_____-_____

I. THE MEMBERS OF YOUR OWN FAMILY

    a. Father & Mother

    b. Father & Mother In Law

    c. Children

    d. Brothers & Sisters

    e. Aunts & uncles

    f. Nieces & Nephews

    g. Cousins

II. YOUR CLOSEST FRIENDS AND THOSE YOU ASSOCIATE WITH ALMOST DAILY

    a. Friends & Neighbors

    b. People with whom you work

    c.   People with whom you spouse works

    d.   Members of your Church or Sunday school Class

III.   THOSE YOU HAVE MET IN ORGANIZATIONS OR CLUBS

    a.   Church Members

    b.   Civic Groups, Rotary, Exchange, JC's, Kiwanis

    c.   Political Groups

    d.   Lodge, Elks, Moose

    e.   Missionary Societies & Brotherhood Groups

    f.   Merchants or Farm Organizations

    g.   School Groups, Booster, PTA, etc.

IV.   THOSE YOU HAVE BEEN ASSOCIATED WITH IN THE PAST

    a.   Schoolmates (use school yearbook)

    b.   Former job associates

    c.   People in your former town

    d.   College Mates

    e.   Army Buddies

V.   THOSE WITH WHOM YOU DO BUSINESS (FROM WHO YOU BUY)

    a.   Doctor, Lawyer, Barber, Merchants, Grocer

    b.   Gas Station, Laundry, Milkman, Insurance Man

    c.   Beauticians, Jewelers, Favorite Restaurants

    d.   Anybody with whom you do business

VI.   LIST OF ACQUAINTANCES ALREADY AVAILABLE
   a.   Christmas card list
   b.   Church Directory
   c.   Civic Club Membership
   d.   Small town phone book

As you can see they really want you to sell on the practice demo as its not only a huge confidence boost to you, as you can yes do this. It costs them nothing to pay you when you sell and they make money at the same time so they are very happy for you to sell to those who trust you.

DEFENDER FILTER COST

Initially at my training there was no mention of the defender filter cost and after seeing he who would be my distributor make someone feel very small for asking a question. I declined to inquire I found out later it was around $120 for the white filter and 20-40$ for the charcoal filter. During my presentations I would combine the filter cost and break it down to a daily total and ask if that was reasonable for clean air. People agreed and I had covered the filter cost. About a year into the employment I remember Dominic flipping out at sales staff for not mentioning the filter cost. I declined again to inform him he left it out as did others but he must have been getting the first few services done and the service sales person was getting a hard time selling filters. As the customers were later shocked to find out that there was a cost associated with replacement filter. It was mentioned during my training we would be going back to change the filters as the sales rep ourselves so I also relayed what would again turn out to be false information, until I figured out it was not me myself going back but another individual would be doing that later.

DOMINIC'S DEMO

This demo was early on in my experiences with this company it was to a couple in Fredericton who purchased on the spot like many would and then cancelled later on as many would also do. This I found out on my pay cheque as Dominic told me before the demo that if he sold we would split the commission what a nice guy….. Come pay day and no pay other then my other job other then the bare minimum which the sales manager at the time fought for me to get, as he wasn't planning on issuing that to me and subsequently a time or two afterwards he did not.

TRADE IN VACUUM CLEANER

During the presentation at the end, the sales person will offer to buy your old vacuum this is for a few reasons.One you get a discount today and only today because you viewed the presentation, no pressure though. Another reason is to remove that unit from your home so you don't go back to your comfort zone and use it and worst of all return the new product you invested in. Finally it's just another income stream as I witnessed at least twice once in the office at new Maryland highway another at Union Street. Once it was a gentleman from Saint John who purchased a bulk load of used vacuums and another was a lady in Fredericton who ran a used vacuum cleaner store.

WORKING TWO JOBS

Prior to leaving the call center I was employed at gainfully, I was moon lighting there to pick up some pay for bills as I was selling a fair number of machines but the customers were being rejected by the finance companies. So as I had agreed to stay on in a limited capacity to help get sales at the call center on their DSL program in my available time and I was able to make ends meet for a while. And I was content with that then one day I was told in the filter queen morning meeting we were going on a road crew today to go home pack your suitcases and there you go. I could no longer moonlight and was now forced to rely solely on my filter queen income for my obligations.

ROAD CREWS

Be prepared as the scouts say, for quite a few surprises one of which was never mentioned to me was this concept of road crew i.e. leave your home go to a hotel or other accommodations which you also pay for in addition to your normal housing costs and gasoline. You have limited options for cooking and are constantly eating out. Far from any support network you have which might help illuminate your path of choice at the present time is more futile then you would otherwise think.

That idle time you know your rest and relaxation time is pressured into posting flyers sending fraudulent mail outs, meaning the prizes listed available are not in fact available. If you're not generating leads your taking them down so people can go to their demos all of which is "earn and learn aka un paid time". There is a lot of that unpaid time in this field so much it almost reminds me when I was a volunteer leader. Only difference is it didn't cost me much to volunteer with the scouts compared to this company.

CHIPMAN MINTO ROAD CREW

This was to be my first big expensive employment venture. We stayed at a hotel at a cost, it was all this earn and learn stuff you'd hear and how generous our contractor was to pay 50% of the cost of the hotel what a nice guy. Well this hotel was kind of funny as it still had train tracks behind it which were in use, so I asked the folks I was travelling there with if they had ever been to a place that had beds that shake after you put some quarters in them, no one had. They asked why and I said you'll find out later as I knew there would be a train sometime in the night and the head of the bead was next to the wall which was about 20 -30 feet from the train tracks. The next morning at breakfast in the hotel not split 50%50 this was my food so it was on me to pay it. Well it was quite funny for me as I got some dirty looks and some folks said "we know what you mean now".

WORK SMARTER NOT HARDER.

How often I would hear this but I don't think mentally I've ever worked so hard in my life then this time at healthy living home ltd. The first time was out in the office in New Maryland just outside Fredericton and it made sense like all things do in the moment in hindsight though. I was marketing, selling, processing financial applications driving and being micromanaged at all times to do those tasks. Or you would be running to get more free gifts for the company to hand out aka Tide. Never once was I reimbursed gas for picking up tide products as in gas money or time money, Dominic paid for the tide.

PERTH ANDOVER ROAD CREW

This road crew during winter would prove to be annoying on a few occasions, one during a winter storm I refused to take my car on the unsafe roads between the sales manager and the distributor and another sales rep offering their CRV for the experience I went. I don't remember how I got conned into that one but I should have realized then how little my life was valued by this company but I went and almost made it into the ditch but was able to get to the presentation and did not sell, and made it back to the hotel only worse for wear in spirits. Another situation came about when we arrived I arrived to a single bed hotel room and was informed I'd be sharing the bed I felt bad for the rep sleeping on the floor that night but there was no way I was paying to share a bed. Meeting the tucker from hell at the VLT was just icing on the cake for this we scored a small amount of cannabis He wanted to sell stuff all right and not just cannabis nor small amounts of it either. He got very insistent and belligerent. We managed to exit the cab of his truck by offering to return with more beer, no one went back with beer and I'm sure everyone involved in that truck cab from the sales side locked their doors that night.

USING ME AS A RECRUITMENT TOOL

When Dominic had discovered that my former place of employment had closed he utilized that in his interview process by hinging on the 80+ years of service from filter queen with no lockouts or shutdowns. I did not mind being a recruitment tool as I was so I thought building my future in fact I was not as it turned out.

VIDEO LOTTERY TERMINAL RAGE SESSION

During the Perth Andover road crew on off time we would conglomerate around the bar area of the hotel and this time one night we were there. I witnessed someone put their whole pay into the machine and it did not pay out at all. So this Lady who was playing the VLTS took it out on the machine this was the first time I ever experienced such brutality toward a machine she was removed and banned for a while from the premises.

WOODSTOCK ROAD CREW

Another Learn to earn experience again the hotel was split 50/50 cost wise which again is an additional cost if you were going to be away from home base. This motel had a German style restaurant in it so at least I found the food nice but too pricey so I ate there once or twice. Paying normal bills plus hotel expenses, left little for enjoyment. Also the phone bill at the time had increased dramatically I'd be called at all times when done a demo for another or for putting out flyers or a meeting back at the hotel so there was little time to begin with. I found it mentally relaxing to shine my shoes I always did, so I shined others for free sure I could have charged them but while I was shining shoes I did not have to engage in more frivolous conversation about work and could instead be lost in the magically world of working with my hands. it was here I would be introduced to VLT's a sales person put 20 $ in and said hit this button and of course it wins $150 or so. I think I came close to breaking even playing VLTS overall but it was not a great expenditure of my time but the meeting place would almost always be a bar or so as that's where others conglomerated and as such I would too.

GREAT MAJESTIC OF FIRE

This one demo I was doing the vacuum cleaner caught on fire blue flames were protruding from the motor cover. Thankfully I saw it because normally the air sample is done in a bedroom and we moved outside on their deck after the fire. They were interested in the machine enough to buy a new one out of the box after the full presentation. I said you know they make a lot of these machines there's bound to be one unlucky such person to get one and demo it but that's why they give you a 5 year warranty on the motor and they were happy enough with that explanation. So while waiting for Tim to bring a new machine for me to demo we finished the air purifier presentation. I did the trading call and they were dumbfounded I still sold the machine which was confusing as I was really new at the time and I thought everyone wanted one after the demo for the most part they said they did, and if you could fit it into their budget they would purchase it.

MEETING THE BOSS'S BOSS HIS UNCLE

Further cementing the image of a family business one that cares about health more than wealth and its ok to get wealthy while helping others stay healthy or so you are sold on. That said this individual would appear more than once to the office and offer kind words of encouragement to me and others also he would showcase the success of the business model. I would receive mail from this individual personalized and it sucked me in even more to this organization in hind sight it was only more manipulation some good cop bad cop.

www.filterqueen.org

Dominic Soffee
President of Sales
New World Division

Phone : +1.905.565.0068 Mobile: +1.416.576.1939
Fax   : +1.905.565.0076 Email: dsoffee@fqcda-intl.c

TRIAL BUY VACUUM

MCADAM

During this not road crew we would drive 74.5km each day from the capital and then some demos would be another hour away from that and the price of gas was a real hardship. Also the time well that was learn and earn right, driving did not seem to count towards your job here often it would be repeated you are just driving. It was after this road crew I and others were called on by Mr Tahhan to go to court to testify to the terms and conditions of our employment. Anyway it must not have been going his way as they settled outside of court.

SECONDARY FINANCING

After being employed /contracted by Healthy Living Home ltd for a while Dominic obtained a secondary finance company, which we could use if the primary finance company rejected the application. I was doing a presentation to a couple out in Mcadam and they were interested in 2 defenders and one majestic normally that would have been around a 1000 $ commission check. I did get paid 100$ and was told I should be thankful I got anything as normally it would have been a rejected sale. I was silently furious as that just covered gas and food for the day. Nor was I in a position to reject the meager $100.00. I did find out later on as I climbed the ranks and thru listening that the distributor made substantially more than $100.00 from a secondary finance deal and that was a factor in my later assessment of this man of his word.

EXPEDIENCE

Hurry up constantly I would be told to hurry up while driving on the road your guess is as good as mine if he wanted me to drive faster than the speed limit. That sure seemed to be the inclination and at sometimes I got so annoyed with it all I did and then I got caught. Once and did not speed much anymore and the hurry up continued on the phone.

THEORETICAL RECRUITMENT OF KAREN

During one Road crew in Grand falls, I had an idea which I discussed with Tim. We both thought it was a decent idea as we were independent contractors we were going to sub contract out demos to a local person or persons. Then we were going to pay them a commission structure we had devised. I had one such person of interest identified, Karen which I had met somehow recently. She was interested in the product and showed some interest in selling them. So after collecting the information and arriving at her place to do a presentation to recruit her I observed there was a young months old baby on the table. That was enough for me to dive the recruitment attempt as she was a single mother who was having a time of life as it was, and I had already had my suspicions about my boss at the time. With the slightly more limited commission it would have been harder for her to make ends meet than her current circumstances provided. So I went back to the House at this time after much insisting we rented a house as it was cheaper and more convenient then a hotel I mean I could cook some meals, have a shower get the demos at 9 or so am hand them out to all the staff that was there then go to my demo. Be prepared to be honest and trustworthy kind and cheerful considerate and clean and wise in the use of all recourses. And I did my best to stay true to my scouting mentorship from my youth. It was not always easy and I did not always succeed one person I was supposed to pick a defender up but after being sent 100km away from her place. Then called to go pick it up and then go to a demo 50 km in the other direction I said nope you do it hung up the phone. Then I did the demo and stopped thinking about it because not having enough money for gas and food at the time I had other concerns like running out of oil in the house in Fredericton. Where I had a mortgage and my partner soon to be fiancée who had no heat, and I wasn't even allowed to go home according to the boss as I needed to be in Grand falls. Luckily my father was in close proximity so I got him to put some diesel in the tank for a night or two until payday and I could afford the 600$ of oil. I neglected to go pick it up that defender and the boss did not seem to care until a year later when it was time to change the filters. Also contributing to stresses the distributor withheld funds from your paycheck his words were "I'm not paying you all that money you'll just spend it, it's for a rainy day" He would of course pay those funds at a later date but sometimes then you were late paying your bills.

CELL PHONE OF CONTROL

I hate phones now I don't even have a personal phone my wife does and that suffices for the calls we need to make. After wearing a headset for 3 years and then being manipulated via phone for 2 and some more plus witnessing the gross misrepresentation of information to my peers in order to turn them into prospects I grew to detest them. My distributor would call on time designated as off for demos or to pickup tide for him or to stick flyers on doors or mailboxes all for his business, at me and my colleges expenses this was considered learn and earn. The times my wife would have my phone when she was shopping for her wedding gear would prove intrusive annoying and frustrating for her, as he would demand to know where I was when she would be home and other probing questions.

BRIEF INTRODUCTION OF MY WIFE INTO THE BUSINESS

My wife former fiancée and before that partner who I met before filter queen would prove to be ill equipped for this FAMILY business. I was ill prepared for such questions as "why do you love her" and to find out he would ask her the same thing of me and try and manipulate her as well. The only good thing about the filter queen experience for my wife I believe was when I proposed to her at the Orlando convention in Florida which was by my design as her parent's winter there. So we would spend an extra few days after the convention there, it was when we got back that's when I found Tim in Edmonton and I was more than annoyed when I was told things were "too tight" and Dominic would grasp his neck for emphasis to open another office, here is the problem I had I was done the edge ready to sell vouchers Tim as he arrived a month or few after me in employment was not far behind me but he had an office and I had to wait I was perplexed and this lead to quit #2

HEAD OFFICE VISIT TO FREDERICTON

There was an occasion that Dan Duggan came to Fredericton with Dominic Soffee for a visit Dan was with the parent company that manufactures the products it was a pleasant enough meeting. This reinforced the appearance of professionalism at this point in time. We would meet him again later in Orlando as that was coming up rather soon.

TRIP TO GRAND FALLS HOSPITAL

During the road crew in Grand Falls where we rented a house, I had developed a bulge on my forehead. Later on I'd find out it was a cyst during another road crew in Woodstock months later. The thing that annoyed me more then not being able to get service in my language at 10 pm that night, was that I was unable to take time off for my health to get checked up when they had English personnel there on day staff. So I went that night after it developed into the size of a golf ball hanging partially over my eye inhibiting driving as it was difficult to see out of part of that eye, and to my surprise my bilingual province had no bilingual doctors on staff. After much translations and talking with hands and expressions and the like I provided my medical card. Tim and I sat in the waiting room for what seemed like ever, then I got to see the doctor for 5 minutes I tried explaining in English and my limited French she observed the big bulge and provided a anti inflammatory drug prescription which I took to the drug store the next day, to get filled while on way to you know a demo. There was no time off on road crews. And the promised time off after the road crews seemed to dissipate from a week to 3 or 4 days very quickly. I recall being sent out on a presentation one Sunday it was a "must go" after 1 or 2 days just as road crew had ended. So a real nice house in Lincoln by the water I was sent too it was a mansion and I was tired I showed up said hello here is your tide and have a great day. I was floored he would send me out after I had told him I was inebriated around 8 am and this was 10:15 he called for a 10:30. At this time he had a staff of many he could have called but he chose lucky me. This was after a month where I sold a lot of units so many units he had extra to pilfer from my sales book, to assign to other reps so they could get the free system to sell to pay their way to florida for the convention

GRAND FALLS THE GREAT HORSE ESCAPE

This presentation would be delayed a bit as while I was driving to the prospects house I would be surrounded by horses that escaped their enclosure. I called the office to let them know and it was suggested I honk my horn and go thru I rather enjoyed the view and stayed put until the horses moved on, it was only a few more minutes at that point and they were beautiful. I was getting tired of acting as a sales manager for free and wanted a bit of a break I already had my 20 units sold for that month. As the convention was coming up and that was the goal if you stepped up on the Edge you got a free majestic and defender to sell which would pay your way to Florida.

ADAM NESS

FRENCH DEMOS

After Brittany left and then Jason later on there was no French staff at all at this company yet they would still book French demos. Ironically I had several learn French CD's for the car I would listen too while driving (there was a lot of driving always). So I learnt some language instead of sales techniques for a while also My wife being French and me learning on the PC Prior to working at healthy living home I had some limited knowledge of the language.

FRENCH TEACHER MAJESTIC SALE

This was probably my funniest hardest most rewarding presentation, the couple were a Husband who was unilingual French, and the lady of the house was a Teacher who spoke English I believe fluently. I did the whole presentation as best to my ability in French using English where my vocabulary failed me, and she would translate to her husband those occurrences. There was a lot of animation in the presentation I always did my best to make connections and so people could understand what I was saying or doing. Knowing people are both audio and visual I used both and where one was not sufficient I tried to make up for it with the other. This sale was a huge boost to my confidence I had done something new to me I sold in another language. I got a hard time on the trading call because it was a few hundred less then asking price. I felt good after the conclusion of the presentation a mountain had been climbed and I would be sent on further French presentations. Much to my folly this motivation would carry me for more months in this field of air quality.

OWN WHAT YOU SELL

I used to read sales books a lot of them by famous authors on the discipline and I found them indispensable. One such book had the idea in it that you should own what you sell if you are confident in the product. So an opportunity arose for that development to take place for me in Grand falls. A salesperson had previously purchased the combo for the commission as they were not having many sales at the time. I felt bad when I found out he had purchased the machines for the pay cheque as that meant he was indebted to the finance company for around $4000.00 for the commissions for those machines. In Grand falls this salesperson asked around if anyone wanted t o purchase his majestic and defender he offered a price and I negotiated with him a little and we agreed then I owned machines with no warranty a majestic which we still use to this day, and a defender air purifier which I will never buy a filter from Dominic to replace the original one in the machine.

THE VANISHED PROMISE OF TIME OFF

After a road crew you were supposed to get a week to eleven days or so off from presentations as you had just worked 30+ days nonstop outside of your home city. After Grand Falls we was one such time off period my phone started ringing after day 2 at home for demos. I was floored I couldn't believe I had just spent 30 days or more away and having reached the company goal of stepping up on the Edge program, I was more than annoyed at this betrayal of respecting my time. So back on demos I went I did manage to get 2 more days off to which I was made to feel small and ungrateful for the total of 4 days I did have off.

DOG TREATS

I figured out a cool idea as having had a dog in my youth so I thought that it might be a good idea to carry a few dog treats on me. This was beneficial to me on several occasions making friends with their best friend wasn't even the concept at the time, I would toss a few dog treats if a dog was around once I got asked how I made it too the door. There was a big shaggy dog tied to a leash which did not quite reach to the door but it came very close, I threw treats until the customer came and they were surprised to see me but quite happy to let me do this presentation they said "you're the first sales man to make it in here ".I felt honored and had a lot of fun with them and the presentations we had coffee and it was a pleasant experience.

SACRIFICE

Often you would be told to put your family on the shelf you would be able to take care of them better after you focused on getting your office. So I and others sacrificed family time, friend time. Time, I missed my father's 50th Birthday while on a road crew to sacrifice for this dream which turned into a nightmare. In my opinion it was a form of manipulation intended to separate you from others who may convince you on another form of employment or to give you time to contemplate how it's not working according to that slide you saw on the interview and search for a job on your own. Missing my Dad's 50th birthday was a painful miss for me I prioritized finishing the Edge success program as quick as possible so I would have the time to spend with my family. To many of my friendships it was like I dropped off the planet. Far from my true friends and family not this pseudo surrogate one which appeared as a way of life not just a job but in reality, it turned out to be parasitic in nature and offered little and took a lot of time and in the end expense to pursue.

WINTER CAR CRASH AND QUIT TIME ONE

This one winter there was a storm like we have in New Brunswick Canada one where you can still drive if you have to but it is not recommended. So I refused to go on a presentation due to only having all season tires on my vehicle and not winter tires which are different. Also there was about 3 feet of snow in the driveway and I was removing it. So onwards to the goal of owning my own distributorship I go despite the risks not only to my vehicle but my personal well being. I never made it too that presentation, instead I came to an icy part of the road and lost control on a straight stretch of road and went off of it into the ditch and hit a culvert in the driveway head-on. The Air bags deployed and all I recalled for a few minutes was whiteness everything was white, and bright and then dark then I came too and got out called the office and said I just had an accident I'm calling the tow truck I'm done. Tim arrived shortly after thankfully to pick me up and take me to my father's where the car was towed and I remember calling my now wife from Tim's

car in tears informing her we just lost our only method of transportation which was gifted to us by her parents. She asked if I was ok to which I replied I am but the car is not. Then after paying the nice tow truck driver with my visa card because I was that poor. I had no other funds in the account to pay for things other than credit at that time, I went home. To my absolute horror dismay surprise and anger MR Tahhan showed up unannounced at my door and proceeded to inquire why I would quit now being so far on the Edge to success. A car was only a thing and he knew a relative or friend of his at the O'Leary car dealership in Fredericton and would get that sorted. Furthermore as I had mentioned I was done I quit the gas prices were unreal and the insurance and everything else went up with this profession of choice. To which he replied you'll be in the office now training people not driving your car to demos riding with them to show them how to do it a few times then training a new class. Fool me once well this was the second time I bought a verbal contract of misinformation form this individual.

Bob's Towing Ltd.
LOCAL AND LONG DISTANCE TOWING

485 Canada Street
Fredericton, N.B. E3A 4A8
Bus: (506) 472-5263 Fax: (506) 452-2835
Cell: (506) 461-4693 Res: (506) 472-1469

CUSTOMER _Adam Ness_ ☎ 471 3500

VISA 4535 1035 7044 7019 01/10 x Adam N.

DATE	YOUR ORDER NO.	INVOICE #	TERMS
		10571	NET 10 DAYS

DESCRIPTION	AMOUNT
Towed Alero from The Royal Rd to 2428 Hanwell	
Car went off The Road into The Ditch and Hit a P. Pel and Landed on a Driveway	$120.00
	GST $16.80
Lic # GFN 520 Alero HST# 140658634 TOTAL DUE	$136.80
Crown Victor	

TRIAL BUY VACUUM

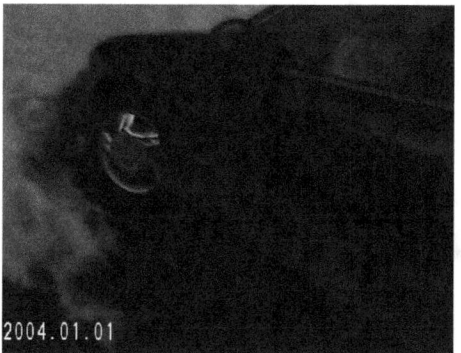

SNOW BOARDING

I had this snow board for years and I never got to use it but I did go this winter we offered to take the fella who was servicing the machines with us a nephew of my boss you know family business thing. He came along with my sister her husband and my fiancé to the Mactaquac ski hill outside Fredericton. It was not a experience I would repeat more than one more time as I found I had less control and without time to get the hang of it I was dangerous on this after almost coming into contact with the same lady on the same run two times.

JEMSEG AREA

This area was almost close to the area I was informed I'd be working in at the start I had just given up on getting local presentations at this point. You went where you were sent and that was it. You went 3 times a day which for me meant I was out most of the day as this was a 43 minute drive from Fredericton. A sad reality that hit often at this point was this was ½ way to my grandparents place. Who I had hardly seen as I was sacrificing for my career in the hopes of having that family time to spend with them.

THE CHOKING

Mr Malcolm was late to his demo, and was rude when he did arrive 25 -30 minutes after I had been there, this time I used to converse with his wife about ironically a family connection. I did a air sample and started to explain the defender air purifier. So when he walked thru the door I believe the first thing he said was where is my tide!? And I replied as per the company policy you get your free gift of tide after giving me your opinion on the products, I was not rude but I was genuine I only had 3 bottles a day and Mr Malcolm lived about 70km from Fredericton so I was more than willing to give him his tide laundry deterrent when we were done. I was mostly done at that time I no longer cared so much about selling the vacuum at that point I just wanted to get out as his veins were popping and his face was getting a shade of red I did not care to see. So after we discussed the situation we arrived at conclusion there would be no more presentation and he would not get his tide for not giving me his opinion on the product. I proceeded to pack up my belongings the demo kit and what not put it all in the bag and box. Walked out the door Malcolm decided to escort me outside and then started threatening me while I was putting stuff in my trunk. When I was finished I turned around to go to my driver's door and as I did so he grabbed my tie and choked me with it forcibly, while his wife was yelling at us both I was just trying to leave I think I kicked him in the shin or wriggled away and got away and yelled something rude to him as I got in my car. At that point I did not care and you know your life is only worth so much I called the office outside in my car on my drive back to Fredericton. After I got the nice lady who answered the phones I explained I would be unavailable for the rest of the day after I told her what had just transpired seconds ago. She passed the phone line to the boss's phone as per normal operating procedure, the distributor the person who's supposed to help you succeed tries to pass me off on another demo, yells at me a bit until I agree to go to on 6:30 but not 3:30. Yes my 11:30 was getting choked causing all sorts of nervousness and uneasy feelings about my choice of career, but the last thing you were accorded was much time off as then you may leave.

THE PONTIAC G6

This car I never wanted I was pressured into purchasing to showcase the success I had as a manager for him and only him but I would pay the bills. His relative/friend at the dealership was already ready with the paperwork when we arrived. Yes Mr Tahhan came with me I had no vehicle and was not even afforded a day or two to source a new one. No indeed there is little critical thinking time in this profession, and the concept and only reason I surrendered to purchase this car was not because Brittany had one,..Alas because I was in so deep and I was to be in the office doing training, trading calls, etc, putting out fires... right that lasted 3 weeks. I was not good at it honestly I was In a position to cover up other peoples mistakes lies etc and, it was more unhealthy then working in a call center with a headset on hearing air horns and "get a real job all day!"

I hated this car every day it reminded me of the loss of the previous car. Had I been more firm on refusing to go or if my employer had a shred of decency he never would have asked me to go during unsafe conditions. Also it consumed way more petrol the the Alero we had, the insurance was more tires were more everything was more to operate it money wise.

TRIAL BUY VACUUM

ADAM NESS

O LEARY
PONTIAC - BUICK - GMC LTD.

1135 HANWELL ROAD
FREDERICTON, NB E3C 1A5
Telephone (506) 453-7000
FAX (506) 459-5755
Email: olearypontiac@gmcanada.com
Website: www.olearypontiac.gmcanada.com

HST# 103986568 RT

31899

MONTH	DAY	YEAR
JAN	10	2008

SECTION A: PURCHASER

PURCHASER: ADAM SCOTT NESS
OCCUPATION:
ADDRESS: 60 ROCHESTER ST
APT #:
CITY: FREDERICTON
PROVINCE: NB
POSTAL CODE: E3B 4T1
AREA CODE / PHONE (Res.): (506) 471-3500
PHONE (Work): (506) 458-2390
FAX:
DRIVER'S LICENSE #:
INSURANCE CO.:
POLICY #:
EXPIRY DATE:
INSURANCE AGENT: RBC GENERAL INS COMPANY

SECTION B: VEHICLE DESCRIPTION

NEW ☐ DEMO ☐ USED ☒ OTHER ☐
YEAR: 2005
MAKE: PONTIAC
MODEL: G6
COLOUR: SILVER
VIN: 1G2ZG528454139958
LICENSE #:
STOCK #: 270263A
MOTOR VEHICLE INSPECTION DATE:
IF MANUFACTURER'S WARRANTY APPLICABLE, TIME IS MEASURED FROM: 00 19 0
DISTANCE TRAVELLED: 133325
KM ☐ MILES ☐
PURCHASER'S INITIALS: AN
EXTENDED WARRANTY OFFERED ( ) REJECTED ( )

SECTION C: TRADE-IN DESCRIPTION AND LIEN DISCLOSURE

The Purchaser covenants, represents warrants and agrees to and with the Vendor that: (a) The Purchaser certifies, warrants, covenants, and represents the within statements, information, representations and warranties relating to the trade-in vehicle to be true and complete in every respect and acknowledges that they are material and fundamental to and conditions of this trade-in purchase and that the Vendor relies on them and the Purchaser intends the Vendor to act upon them and acknowledges that the Vendor intends to sell or lease the trade-in motor vehicle; and (b) the Purchaser covenants, warrants, represents and agrees that all warranties and conditions, statutory or otherwise, express or implied, including all implied warranties of merchantability, quality, condition and fitness for purpose, and all remedies and rights of action, including the right to recession, available at law apply to this trade-in Purchaser by the Vendor and that all defects in the trade-in motor vehicle, its equipment or parts, of which the Purchaser is aware of ought to be aware have been fully disclosed and set out herein, that the trade-in motor vehicle conforms with its description, that it is of merchantable condition and quality and that it is fit for all purposes for which such motor vehicle are used.

WAS VEHICLE PREVIOUSLY USED AS A TAXICAB OR POLICE VEHICLE? YES ☐ NO ☒
YEAR:
MAKE:
MODEL:
VIN:
LICENSE #:
YEAR OF ISSUE:
ENGINE #:
NET AMOUNT OF LIEN:
OWED TO:
DISTANCE TRAVELLED:
KM ☐ MILES ☐
HST REGISTRANT #:
HST DUE ON TRADE-IN:
LAST REGISTERED OWNER:
OWNER'S ADDRESS:
OWNER'S SIGNATURE X:

SECTION E: VENDOR AND PURCHASER ACCEPTANCE

The undersigned Purchaser offers and agrees: (1) to purchase from the Vendor the property described in Section B; (2) for the Purchase Price specified in Section X; (3) subject to the adjustments specified in Section D; (4) upon payment terms specified in Section D; upon and subject to: (5) the general terms and conditions specified on the back of this page; and (6) the Vendor's Covenants and Warranties specified below; and (7) the Manufacturer's Warranty contained in Section X; and (8) the Purchaser's covenants, representations and warranties contained in Section C. The Vendor covenants, represents, warrants and agrees to and with the Purchaser that : (a) the Vendor is duly incorporated or continued, organized and validly existing under the laws of its jurisdiction or incorporation; (b) the Vendor has all necessary power, authority and capacity to own and sell the Vehicle; (c) the Vendor has all necessary corporate power, authority and capacity to enter into this Agreement and to carry out its obligations and the execution and delivery of this Agreement and the consummation of the transactions contemplated have been duly authorized by all necessary corporate action on the part of the Vendor (d) the Vendor will be entitled to dispose of the Vehicle at the time of delivery thereof to the Purchaser; (e) the Vendor is a resident of Canada for the purposes of the Income Tax Act (Canada); (f) there are no facts known to the Vendor which should be disclosed to the Purchaser in order to make any of the representations and warranties contained in this Agreement not mislead or which may have a materially adverse affect on the operations of the Purchaser as they relate to the Property.

OFFER: Subject to the terms and conditions contained herein, the Purchaser makes this Offer on

DATE: 01/10/08 X PURCHASER'S SIGNATURE X CO-SIGNER X WITNESS

ACCEPTANCE: Subject to the terms and conditions contained herein, the Vendor accepts the Purchaser(s)'s Offer.

DATE: 01/10/08 X VENDOR'S SIGNATURE X WITNESS

CONDITIONS ON REVERSE FORM PART OF THIS AGREEMENT

SECTION D: VEHICLE OPTIONS & PURCHASE PRICE

#	OPTIONAL EQUIPMENT	LIST PRICE
	Basic Vehicle	
TOTAL RETAIL PRICE		8800.00
FREIGHT		
TOTAL SALE PRICE		8800.00
TRADE-IN ALLOWANCE		
PRICE AFTER TRADE-IN		8800.00
NB TIRE LEVY		
NB INSPECTION		
EXTENDED WARRANTY		1119.00
ADMINISTRATIVE FEE		299.00
SUB-TOTAL		10218.00
HST SALES TAX		1328.34
A.H. & LIFE		577.88
LICENSE		109.00
GASOLINE		
TOTAL PURCHASE PRICE		12233.22
DEPOSIT CASH ☐ CHEQUE ☐ CREDIT CARD ☐		
BALANCE ON DELIVERY		
LIEN AMOUNT		
AMOUNT FINANCED		12233.22

The deposit is payable within 24 hours of acceptance of the offer by the Vendor to be communicated to the Purchaser, and the balance is payable on the Delivery Date.

SELL THE DREAM

I was instructed to sell the Dream more than the machine to sales reps. The dream was your own business financial freedom ability to retire with residual income from filter sales and services in the the area you were in. Slight problem with that, I believed in the machine but I was living a nightmare in almost every interaction with my distributor and I wasn't lying for him.

WINTER TOW, A MUST GO

This one storm I had to shovel snow a lot of it there half a meter or so in the drive way so out I went shoveling to clear the way. Understand we were renting the basement out too so we were responsible for snow removal so our tenant could get out. I had met our tenant at a previous job and then at Filter queen. It sucked I wasn't able to finish shoveling before Mr Tahhan showed up with his truck and a rope and he insisted I was taking too long and I had to go on this demo. He pulled my car out of the snow before I was done leaving my wife to finish snow removal while I went on this demo. I felt bad about leaving the rest for my wife to do but there really was no choice in this environment.

TRIAL BUY VACUUM

QUEST FOR RING

My wife, girl friend at the time and I despite the inappropriate probing questions from Dominic was progressing nicely. And I had decided that at the upcoming Filter Queen Convention I would propose to her, for that I needed a ring. It was a battle to get 1 day off to look for a ring but I did he demanded to see it when I had it. I don't know if he thought I was doing something other then ring shopping but it seemed like he was more interested in me doing a demo then taking care of important personal business.

FILTER QUEEN CONVENTION 80TH YEAR ORLANDO FLORIDA

My now wife, then girlfriend and I had a decent enough time at the convention. I had found out prior to us going we were to appear on stage for some award for our sales efforts. I had mentioned That I would of liked that time to propose to my wife, both Dominic Soffee and Dominic Tahhan talked me out of that. So I would propose to her at night in a suite in the Marriott world center hotel in Orlando Florida

QUIT TWO AFTER CONVENTION

This time I quit 1 day after returning from the Filter Queen convention in Florida. I returned one week later as I had proposed during a night meeting at the convention to my wife in front of a lot of local staff, my boss his boss (his uncle) and staff from other offices in N.B... She said yes and then we spent some time at her parents for a week in Florida as they winter there. Again I had had enough lies. The proof was in the pudding Tim was moved to Edmunston New Brunswick running a satellite office for Mr Tahhan and his company Healthy living homes LTD. I was ready to sell vouchers for my office in Bathurst to which when I did make the first sale I said that's one on the trading call and then MR Tahhan proceeded to give me verbal abuse over the phone for about 5 minutes while I was in the customer's home in Linclon just outside Fredericton. They heard him screaming his head off at me and asked what that was about I don't remember what I told them something about a pay discrepancy I think. So it was after that abuse that I went right back to the office and I was more than annoyed with the abuse I just got also I had no machines as I had sold both the majestic and defender at this presentation so I would need a new set. So he gave me more verbal abuse about how I don't get to go to my office or sell my vouches he then told me things are too tight financially right now and I won't be able to open my office. I handed him his demo kit and went home, next day that do you think showed up at my door?. Keep in mind at this time I was driving a Pontiac G6 paying obscene gas prices going to presentations well over 75 km from home and in every direction.

So what I was told the first time I quit about training and running the office had been proven false by deeds and time spent. Somehow at my door he managed convince me to come back and my now fiancé would also come work for him for a while. And I am so thankful that was a short transition period for her. She's my wife and I love her and when he started pestering her about why does she love me and saying stuff like you know her problems will rub off on you. My wife has few problems who doesn't, what he neglected to realize or ascertain was that she is French so when English is being spoken fast and furious sometimes she needs it repeated. Well after a few weeks or a month of that she had enough and that was that. She was not working for him and I was back to road crew while I worked at selling my vouchers then I would indeed be able to have my office as per the whole concept of 'contracting myself out'. Rather tho I was becoming an unwitting servant by misinformation and manipulation.

NACKAWICK CUSTOMER REQUESTED A TRUCK FOR THE PRESENTATION

    This customer had requested someone with a 4x4 Truck come to do their presentation that I was sent on. As you know I had a car, I did not have a truck. By the time I had realized what a steep incline their driveway was it was too late I was committed to going down. There was no back up option the roads were ice the driveway no better down was the only way to go. When I arrived they were very friendly and asked how you plan on getting out of here to which I said that's a very good question. They had a four wheeler they would push me up the hill with later, the hill being their driveway. They told me that they had told the office to send someone with a truck and now that I was stuck. I asked if they had any coffee so we did a coffee presentation with the defender they got a few jugs of tide for being super nice people. And I was less than happy with knowing that a truck was requested for very good reason and I was sent regardless of that reason.

DOOR KNOCKING

This was the best way for me to generate leads and sales I had more success knocking on doors then I did from office leads honesty was a big part in that. Introducing myself as Adam from Healthy living home and I had 2 products that could help people who suffered from asthma and allergies and they saved you time and money. I'd like to show them to you and give you a gift of tide for your time.   My belief was I was waging war on unhealthy devices and saving people time and money, time cleaning by doing it once and money by investing in a life time machine.

LETTER FROM DOMINIC SOFFEE

 FILTER QUEEN OF CANADA
INTERNATIONAL

Hello Mr. Adam Ness

Please accept this hand written note as a sincere Congratulations on all your recent winnings of free majestic and Defender plus --- and the recent achievement of being a Role Model one more time in beautiful N.B. as the Champion of Door Knocking

yes Adam you have shown us one more time that you honor your word and that is rare in today's world.

you know so much about the Art of Selling Adam and your real mission have just started, the door knocking test that you are going through successfully is a good sign of great things to happen for you and your team in N.B. I will be watching for results.

once again Adam Congratulations on your consistancy in working hard and smart we know that life is what we make it take so let's do it good. See you soon till then keep it up.

Sincerely
Dominic Soffee

6345 DIXIE RD. U#4 • MISSISSAUGA •ON• CANADA L5T 2E6
PHONE: (905) 565-0068 • FAX: (905) 565-0076

TRIAL BUY VACUUM

SELLING THE HOUSE

Before we moved to Bathurst I was informed I could not have a house in Fredericton and run an office in Bathurst at the same time. This would be too much distraction from the office if anything happened to the house and a bunch of other reasons. We decided, Yasmine and I that we were in as deep as we were so as we had decided so many times in the past year and a half that ok we'll sell the house and move to Bathurst. So we did, at less than we could have got had we waited a while longer. At least we did not sell at a loss with a remainder on the mortgage, that was clear and paid only the few thousand 5 or 7 thousand I had racked up on the line of credit during the 1.5 or so years I had worked under the tutelage of Mr Tahhan all because of the dream. Once the house was sold Yasmine my fiancé moved to my mother's for about 5 months while I worked in Bathurst selling the rest of the vouchers and then I finished selling the vouchers. After I had finished selling the vouchers I was out of stock other then 1 unit so in order to keep making money I needed more units or to have those funds from all those machines transferred to my account at TD Bank. Which was the same bank he used for his business so it was going to be a easy process to transfer the funds.

TRIAL BUY VACUUM

PROPERTY FULL VIEW   Page 1 of 2

$5000 CASHBACK FOR DECORATING UPON CLOSING

Price:	$160,000
Status:	Sold

MLS® #:	00896493
PID #:	01469824
File #:	2008155527

Legal Descr.:
Address: **60 ROCHESTER ST**
City: **FREDERICTON, E3B 4T1**

Side of Road:		District:	FRS
Lot Size:	792 SQ M	Sub-Dist:	B1
House Dimensions:	40X24	Zoning:	
Elem Schl:	LIVERPOOL	Occupancy:	Owner
		Sec. School:	ALBERT

List.Date:	10-FEB-2009	Possession:	NEGOTIABLE
Closed:	15-APR-2009		

Overview: Income potential in the ever popular Skyline Acres! This lovely 3+2 bedroom bungalow offers loads of convienence-5 minutes to either up or downtown, close to schools, parks & even a tennis court across the street! Within the last 10 years it has had new siding, windows, exterior doors, oil tank & kitchen added downstairs. Main floor has hardwood in kitchen, dining, bedrooms (3rd bed has carpet covering hardwood). Don`t miss out, this one can potentially help pay the mortgage or be easily converted to a 2 unit student housing! $5000 Cashback to purchaser for decorating

Directions: From Forest Hill, turn onto Canterbury, Rochester Street on the right, go to civic number 60
Show.Instr.: Through Amanda 476-7423

Type:	Single Family	Heating:	Oil, Baseboard, Hot Water	Exterior:	Alum/Vinyl
Style:	Bungalow	Garage Type:	Detached, Double	Driveway:	Double, Paved
Title to Land:	Freehold	Water:	Municipal	Foundation:	Fully Developed
Property Size:	Under 0.5 Acres	Sewer:	Municipal	Features:	
Land Features:	Level, Partial Landscaped	Services:	Electricity, Telephone, Cable, City Bus Service	Roof:	Asphalt Shingle
Access:	Year Round Road Access	Rental Equipm.:	None	Flooring:	Carpet, Cushion/Tile/Lino, Wood

Documents:

Inclusions: Fridge & stove(located in garage), fridge & stove in basement, curtains & rods, 1 garage opener, storage shed (8x8)
Exclusions: Fridge & stove on Main floor, washer, dryer
Remarks: Income potential in the ever popular Skyline Acres! This lovely 3+2 bedroom bungalow offers loads of convienence-5 minutes to either up or downtown, close to schools, parks & even a tennis court across the street! Within the last 10 years it has had new siding, windows, exterior doors, oil tank & kitchen added downstairs. Main floor has hardwood in kitchen, dining, bedrooms (3rd bed has carpet covering hardwood). Don`t miss out, this one can potentially help pay the mortgage or be easily converted to a 2 unit student housing!

Bedrooms:	3+2	Sign:	Yes			Garage: Yes	Gar.Details: 24X26`6
Bathrooms:	2 \	Lockbox:	Yes	SPIS:	Yes	Water Access:	Water:
Rental Income:	POTENTIAL	Road:				Building Colour: WHITE	
Building Age:		On Land Titles:					

Floor	Room	Size	Floor	Room	Size
MAIN FLOOR	LIVING ROOM	16`1X12`11	BASEMENT	KITCHEN	12X10`9
MAIN FLOOR	KITCHEN	10X17`9	BASEMENT	FAMILY ROOM	21`5X10`8
MAIN FLOOR	BATH (# pieces 1-6)	6`5X6	BASEMENT	BEDROOM	7`10X10
MAIN FLOOR	BEDROOM	10`2X9`8	BASEMENT	BATH (# pieces 1-6)	6`5X6
MAIN FLOOR	MASTER BEDROOM	12X10	BASEMENT	BEDROOM	15`10X7
MAIN FLOOR	BEDROOM	9`8X9`10			

Assessment: $		Taxes: $2345 (2008)	Improvements:	
Mortgagee:		Mortg.Rate:	Subj.to Verif.:	
Mortg.Amount: $		Due Date:	Condo Fee:	
Payment (PI): $		Payment (PIT): $	Mobile/Leased Land F:	
Seller Name: **A NESS**		Home Tel.:	Bus.Tel.:	

http://www.filogixdms.com/frnb/view_one/display_property.html?counter=e3662485185...   10/25/2012

ADAM NESS

BEING CALLED BOY

At some point my distributor got the idea in his head to start calling me boy and it annoyed me that he would deviate from my name when I was at that time his top producer. Why he did it I don't know. He probably thought it was funny like he did when he was driving others cars from the back to the front and parking them when his license was suspended at the New Maryland office. "Here is your pay cheque boy" "Come here boy" the list went on "Boy I need tide" Boy I was tired of that.

NO CAR HIRED ANYWAY

This one new hire irked me a lot he had no vehicle and Dominic expected others to drive him to and from demos and I was not having it. I think I took him to 2 or 3 demos my finances were in shambles, I was driving a car I did not want and I didn't have the extra dollars for gas to ferry another person around. The person was like Dominic a recent immigrant. I trained him took him to 2-3 demos after his practice demos some others took him on other demos. I felt bad for the guy he had no sales experience no car and the demos could be quite far he in the end did not stay too long.

OPENING TD BANK ACCOUNT FOR DEPOSITING OF FUNDS FROM VOUCHER SALES

This was a short trip to The Toronto Dominion bank in Fredericton on Westmoreland Street; the drive was agonizing under interrogation by Mr. Tahhan for whatever he felt like harassing me about that day. Then he popped the question of which I rather have In the office with me him or Tim to which I replied Tim to his ire. I parked the car we got out I went and opened an account that was that. We went back to the office and picked up stock to head back to Bathurst N.B. again leaving my fiancé in Fredericton while I chased this dream that was sold to me. It was never my dream but it made sense as they teach you to make sense till it hurts and then ask a close ended question sit and wait for a response in silence. Silence can build a lot of pressure on an person in a demonstration.

THE DRIVE FROM BATHURST TO MY WEDDING IN BOUCTOUCHE

This drive I will never forget so long as I don't contract a problem that makes me do so, It was raining hard I had only driven this particular highway once before I was alone and the windshield wipers stopped working. Being the boy scout I used to be and tried to maintain, I tried a piece of rope to each wiper and made a U shape with the bottom of the U being inside the car so I could manually operate the wipers. While driving with one hand it sucked as the windows were down and I got soaked the car inside got soaked but I made it to my destination the next day I discovered RainX. Which is a product you can apply to the windshield and the rain beads off. I had to take the car the G6 to the Devon auto garage to replace the plastic windshield wiper bar that connected them together as that was not covered by the dealership bumper to bumper warranty. I thought this warranty would cover all but no and so I was out another $300-$400 for that on top of car payments insurance gas and at this time rent, because I was living in Bathurst with Tim.

BEST MAN AT WEDDING WAS A DNS (DOMINIC NO SHOW)

I had asked my Distributor to be the best man at my wedding I was in so deep I had the horse blinders on and was only seeing company information self absorbed towards the goal of financial freedom owing my own office. I would be training professional sales people like a fished fish I was in hook line and sinker. I asked him to be my best man he agreed in company of others. I Found out the day before the wedding he was not coming what a cancelation that was. Thankfully my wife and her parents were leaving that part of the invitation blank and I had a great one of the best people around me Tim, and he would be my best man at the wedding. We had both been thru a lot at filter queen and as they say misery loves company.

3RD AND FINAL QUIT

After I had finished all the training classed prior to moving to Bathurst I noticed on my Webpage from the parent company that I was sent the regional candidate certificate but I never received that certificate from Mr. Tahhan. I suspect it was withheld as I had a meeting with him and his uncle the president of the company in Canada in a week. This meeting was after I had demanded the monies to be deposited in the account I had opened a week prior at TD bank with MR Tahhan. Tim came for the ride to open that account during the drive I was asked who I would rather work with me in my office Tim or Mr Tahhan to which I replied Tim, because together with both of us doing demos and training the office would be better served then by having a remote assistant in Fredericton. This set Mr Tahhan on into a rage saying things like "what do you know about business boy" and other insults. Well the meeting with Mr Tahhan and his uncle the president of the company came and lasted a whole 60 seconds or less. I was sat down waiting as I had been for a while as they were late, then we filed into the office sat down I and Mr Tahhan sat at the reception part of the desk and Mr Soffee behind and I said well what's happening now then, and Mr Soffee said you're not ready yet maybe in another year shook my hand and got up and walked away. That was the last I seen of Mr Soffe. Mr Tahhan got up sat in his chair on his business side of the desk and looked at me I was perplexed. I had completed everything required by the company to receive those monies in my account for my business. That was the dream be your own boss financial freedom I think I may have had a tear in my eye or 2 then and I got up and walked out. I went back to my mother's place where my wife was I informed her and my mother of what had transpired. The next day I marked on a air sample in pen "The Dream has been poisoned" and left it in the majestic unit I returned to him the next night I was done being hoodwinked and tricked. Another year of more lies and falsehoods after we sold our house and completed all the work required, the goal line kept moving and I had enough chasing it we were done. The next picture is a snap shot of the parent companys website that shows I completed the tasks required to open an office

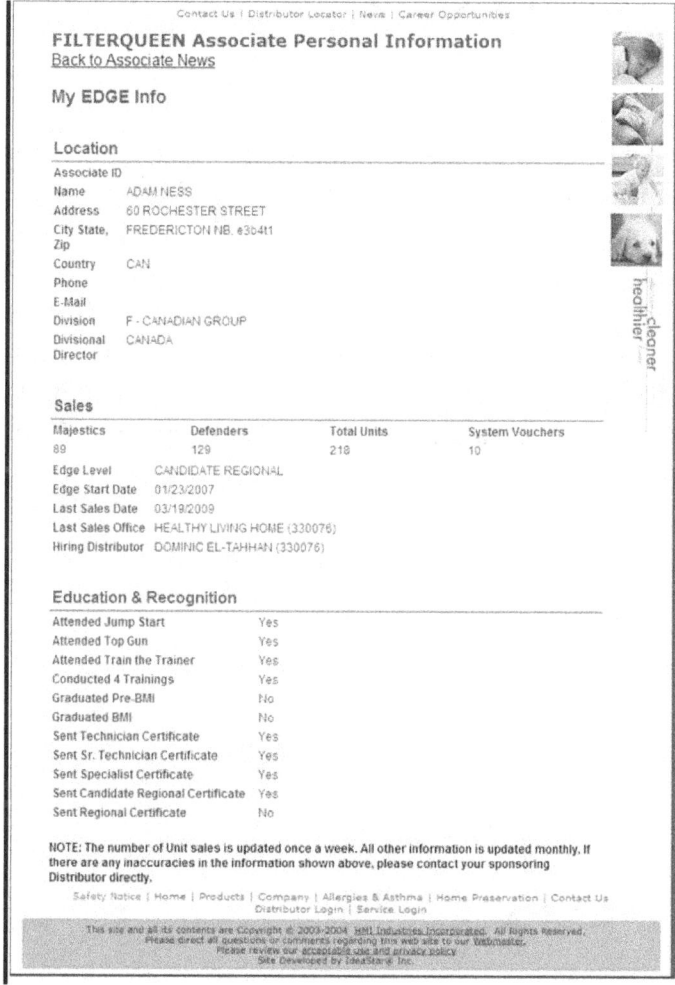

SO BEFUDDLED I THANKED THEM FOR THE HARDSHIP

I was so confused after this whole experience that I even wrote Dominic Tahhan and Soffee an email thanking them for the time allowing me to propose to my wife in Florida. Well I would even visit him in the hospital once when he got accosted later in life, then I found out thru the grape vine that he said I asked for my job back. To which yeah no never again would I submit myself to his con artistry my head could not process information rationally and logically, like it had before this experience but I knew I had enough of it.

POST CHASING THE DREAM NIGHTMARES CAME TO ROOST

I had racked up quite a bit of debt during my tenure, a loan at a bank and my line of credit were maxed out all because I was plugging away for that big payday of getting those vouchers sold. To open my own office and pay off debts the problem as you know is I was never paid for those vouchers.

Being in Bathurst now, My wife sourced a job at Zellers and I at with another cyclonic action vacuum machine. Then the car was destined to be reprocessed as we were unable to maintain the payments. So then I started working at Sears. With the car being gone Bathurst with no public transportation so when winter came with no car and walking to work taking ½ a hour for my wife. With temperatures that reach well below freezing we moved back to Fredericton at my mom's trailer with her for a period of time some dream.

RCMP J DIVISION VISIT

At wits end before trying to sue this individual I just wanted right done not by me or for me but for others. I did not want anyone to go thru what I had So I went and buzzed in at the RCMP HQ and spoke thru their microphone and speaker apparatus on the wall. Sure it was a real person but it was a very impersonal experience. I tried to detail the mail frauds the financial fraud I had gone thru in those 2-4 minutes allotted to speak to me. At the conclusion of this brief visit it was suggested I get a lawyer so that's what I did, albeit to a futile effort.

DEBT COLLECTORS

Due to being unable to meet the repayment terms of these loans I was paying off the compound interest at revenue Canada as a primary payment and the loans as secondary concerns. I had calls many calls not just to us but anyone with my last name in the phone book pretty much got a call looking for me and money from them for my debts. This was too much after finding out about that which was going on for about a month I had little choice but to stop these calls and the only way I knew how to do that was bankruptcy. And then the kind government made it legal for them to call on Sunday too. There's not much to say about the people who called they were less then professional quite rude and it did nothing constructive.

DECEPTION DURING COVID

Although this happened after my time its worth nothing that Healthy Living Home was found out to be lying about their products and covid.... here is the picture taken off the health Canada website.

Summary table of advertising incidents addressed by Health Canada related to COVID-19 as of September 1, 2022

Ongoing | Resolved

Filter items: defender

Showing 1 to 2 of 2 entries (filtered from 560 total entries) | Show 10 entries

Product name / Description	Product type	Manufacturer/distributor involved with non-compliance	Company / Advertising media	Claim
Defender	Medical Device	Yes	Healthy Living Home ltd	COVID-19. is 0.125 micron in size. The Defender filters 99.99% of particles down to 0.1 micron.
Pure Defender Disinfectant	Over The Counter	Yes	Pure Defender Sanitizers Inc. website	It is a Health Canada approved disinfectant that can be used in the fight against COVID-19

CONCLUSION

If You Had To Lie To Hire Me, And Then Had To Lie To Keep Me.
If You Had To Lie To Your Prospects,
What Type Of 'Business' Do You Run?

Who Wants To Be Lied To? And Who Wants To Lie For You?
Are You A Man Of Your Word?
Because As You Can See I Picked Up A Lot Of Dirt.

www.ingramcontent.com/pod-product-compliance
Lightning Source LLC
Chambersburg PA
CBHW050004230526
45465CB00003BB/1251